TAKING CHARGE

Making The Right Choices

Perry M. Smith

AVERY PUBLISHING GROUP INC.

Garden City Park, New York

Cover Design: Rudy Shur and Martin Hochberg
Cover Photo: Ultimate Image
In-House Editor: Diana Puglisi

Library of Congress Cataloging-in-Publication Data

Smith, Perry M. (Perry McCoy)
    Taking charge: making the right choices / Perry M. Smith.
       p. cm.
    Bibliography: p.
    Includes index.
    ISBN 0-89529-383-8 (pbk.) : $10.95
    1. Leadership. I. Title.
HD57.7. S65 1988
658.4' 092--dc19

Printed in the United States of America

10 9 8 7 6 5 4 3

CONTENTS

To Connor, the lovely and talented lady who has shared with me the joys and the heartaches of leadership in so many settings.

ACKNOWLEDGMENTS

Many hundreds of people assisted me in the preparation of this book. First and foremost, I must thank the students of the National War College, the students of the Industrial College of the Armed Forces, and the students from many nations from the National Defense University, who took my courses on executive development and on leadership of large and complex organizations. These mature public servants from five military services, a dozen civilian agencies, and ten foreign nations critiqued my book in manuscript and helped me develop my ideas and clarify and polish my rules of thumb, checklists and case studies.

Second, I must acknowledge the substantive contributions of my guest speakers who shared experiences as they ran some of the largest organizations in this country. John Gardner; former Secretary of the Air Force Verne Orr; Ambassador Bill Harrop; Walt Ulmer, President of the Center for Creative Leadership; General Bob Russ, Commander of the United States Air Force's Tactical Air Command; Lieutenant Generals Bob Springer and Bill Maloney, of the U.S. Air Force and Marine Corps, respectively; Mr. Tom Pownall, Chairman, Martin Marietta Corporation; Mr. Bob Kirk, President, Allied Signal; General Bill Depuy, U.S. Army retired; and Vice Admiral James Stockdale, U.S. Navy retired.

Special thanks are due to Mary McNabb and Yvette Taylor, who took dictation by the hour and who typed the initial manuscript; Patricia Pasquarett, who carried out many typing and editing duties; Cathy Salvato, who accomplished many editorial chores; Sherwood (Woody) Goldberg, who helped restructure the manuscript at a critical phase; and to Fred Kiley, Don

Anderson, Walter "R" Thomas, Laura Conk, Jack Jacobs, Mike Miller, Charlie and Jane Hamm, Bob and Harriet Plowden, Ed Parks, Bill Clover, Jim Simms, Bob Sorley, Buddy Diamond, and Ken Wenker for their substantive and editorial comments.

Thanks are also due to Rudy Shur and Diana Puglisi of Avery Publishing Group. Their helpful suggestions and careful attention to detail were greatly appreciated.

And last but not least, my thanks go to Connor Smith who critiqued and edited the manuscript and put up with a husband who once again was inspired to write and rewrite.

PREFACE

For many years I have been looking for a practical guide for running organizations. Since I was unable to find such a guide anywhere in the literature, I decided to write the guide myself. I did so while serving as the Commandant (and teaching courses on executive development and on leadership) at the senior professional school for career civilian and military officials with the highest potential for leadership, the National War College in Washington, DC.

This book is not a scholarly treatise and it breaks no new conceptual ground on leadership or management. I designed it for the busy leader who might have a few hours free while riding on an airplane or on a quiet Sunday afternoon to get some helpful hints on running his or her organization and on dealing with the tough issues that he or she will face in the days and weeks ahead.

It is also designed for subordinates who must deal with the boss and are interested in understanding the problems and dilemmas that the top executive is facing. In addition, it is designed for use in management and leadership courses to augment the more theoretical works that are available in the literature.

I have had the great pleasure of having been in charge of a number of large organizations as well as a few complex staff directorates. *I have written the book that I would liked to have had when I was in executive positions.* This book offers many rules of thumb, checklists, and case studies to spark the interest of the reader. It is a very personal book; it attempts to incorporate hundreds of insights I have gained over the course of over thirty years while I worked in very large and very complex organizations, here and in five other nations.

The book is designed to allow executives to dive easily into it at a time of need. You are about to hire someone? Go to my hiring checklist. You need to fire someone? Reread the short chapter on firing and glance at the firing checklist. You are frustrated by your meetings? Use the meeting checklist. You are about to take over a big job? The transition chapter may be helpful. Hence, this is both a guide and a handbook.

Leaders count. People at the top can—should—make a difference. Leaders decide whether you can vote, what music you will hear, whether there will be gas at the pump, which neighborhoods will be wiped out by a new highway, and whether you will have to give a blood or urine sample to get—or keep—a job. By setting standards, by establishing and maintaining a network of communications, by nurturing relationships, and by motivating subordinates, a leader molds the daily performance of an organization. Further, a leader can permanently affect an organization by establishing a strategic vision with specific long-term goals and implementation strategies. The future is not already determined. What will happen in the next twenty or thirty years will be, in large part, the consequence of decisions that influential leaders will make within their organizations.

This is not a book about how to run a small office or enterprise. This is a book for leaders and subordinates in *large* or *complex* organizations. *Large organizations* are those with more than five hundred people under the leadership of an individual. Examples include: corporations, both for profit and nonprofit; labor unions; a state, city, or large county (including large police, fire, health, or welfare departments); universities, large hospitals, school systems and large schools; and large military units. *Complex organizations* are those that have such diverse responsibilities that the leader is unable to keep track of all ongoing issues. These complex organizations normally have a hundred or more people. Examples include large staff directorates, research centers, academic institutes, and large embassies.

Leading large and complex organizations requires an approach different from those used in leading smaller organizations. For instance, in large and complex organizations, leaders may not personally know all of their subordinates. Leaders can no longer be specific problem solvers. Communication to the lower echelons becomes much more difficult, and feedback returns through several layers. The intimidation factor of being the "big boss" can impede good communication in both directions. The tendency for the leader to make superficial judgments about the capabilities of individuals often increases. Sycophants who tend to isolate the leader from the important issues or fail to challenge the leader when he has a bad idea are generally more prevalent in large organizations than in small ones. The leader of a large organization has a more difficult and larger role in training other leaders. Greater delegation, trust, empowerment, and loyalty to subordinate leaders are also all at play.

In the last three years of my military career, I had the luxury that few leaders enjoy—the luxury of time: time for reflections, time for teaching, time for research, and time for writing. Teaching a leadership course for three consecutive years to the very best and brightest provided extraordinary insights. In the three years, I taught five seminars. My 136 students came from all the military services of the United States, from many civilian agencies of the Federal Government, and from such nations as Israel, Egypt, the Philippines, Korea, Peru, Great Britain, the Federal Republic of Germany, Jordan, Pakistan, India, and the Somali Republic. Most had already run large or medium-sized organizations, but wanted to learn more and share their insights and ideas (of the international students, one had led an Israeli Army Division into combat in Lebanon, another had been the mayor of a city of 500,000 in the Philippines during the martial law period of Marcos, and another had led a Sikh brigade into the Punjab to root out Sikh terrorists in the trying period of the assault on the Golden Temple at Amritsar in 1984—to name just a few). They all wrote papers, participated actively in the seminar environment, challenged my views, and forced me to revisit, in greater depth, my own experiences as a leader. To have been the Commandant of the great historic national institution, the National War College, and to have had the privilege of teaching such distinguished public servants was a deeply rewarding and uplifting experience. Many of the insights in this book come from this group.

Finally, I had the privilege of interviewing a number of Chief Executive Officers and Presidents of various corporations, banks, schools and universities, and think tanks, to gain their insights into leadership outside the governmental context. These busy leaders had read an earlier version of this book and as a result were able to give me some very specific input on the points that I had raised, the rules of thumb, the checklists, and the case studies. I have listed none of these individuals since I have used a number of their experiences, some of which touch on delicate issues. Of course, I thank them all.

—Perry M. Smith
McLean, Virginia

INTRODUCTION

Running large organizations is challenging work. It also can be rewarding and uplifting. Good management, characterized by sound leadership, judgment, and integrity, is required in virtually any endeavor. Although there are many good books on management as well as leadership, what has been needed is a short, down-to-earth guide for busy leaders to help them cope with the tougher issues.

Perry Smith has written that guide, and leaders and subordinates alike can benefit from his ideas, insights, and rules of thumb. While no magic formulas exist in this area, there is nonetheless a great body of experience upon which one can draw in shaping current and future courses of action.

What is most refreshing about this book is the clarity of language and the crispness of the author's writing style. He gets to his points fast. This is a "tuned in" book. It deals with the real issues, legitimate dilemmas, and myriad possibilities that confront leaders of large organizations. With extensive experience in running such organizations, along with teaching and research in leadership and management, Smith has accomplished what many others would love to have done; he has written a guide that both managers and subordinates can use to be more effective in their professional lives.

There is a deceptive simplicity to this sophisticated volume. In one sense, it is the thoughtful reader's "how-to" book in the field of management. Those of us who have tried to learn plumbing or golf in this manner know it can have its limitations. Nor is it likely that anyone can become master of all he or she surveys in an executive suite as a result of one quick pass through *Taking Charge*.

On the other hand, you have come to the right place if you are interested in a working visit with a talented, knowledgeable, and highly articulate executive who has many valuable perceptions to share. Most important, I believe Perry Smith's ideas are likely to get your own creative juices flowing wherever you reside, or want to reside, in your particular organizational environment. I also think this is the kind of book many readers will want to keep in their libraries and revisit now and again for various aspects of its diverse contents.

Some of his ideas, in fact, invite a double take the first time around. For example, there is the "no nonconcurrence through silence rule," a wonderful way to keep the lines of communication open between a leader and his or her staff. Then there is the "oh by the way problem," alluding to the managerial hazards of snap decisions. By contrast, the "60 percent decision rule" shows the way for managers who tilt toward timidity more often than impetuosity in the decisionmaking process.

Beyond the case studies and checklists, and the chapters ranging from strategic planning to personal introspection, there is also a deeper meaning to all this. We live in an era of unprecedented commercial, technological, and military challenge. We earn our daily bread in an increasingly competitive environment as markets begin to take on truly global proportions. How well we as a nation manage our considerable assets—how effectively our government, industry, and other institutions utilize human and material and financial resources—obviously will be a critical factor in determining our future. It is as simple, and as complex, as that.

Management and leadership skills can be strengthened through learning. In my view, this is a valuable book because it will contribute in a very specific way to developing and honing and refining these essential skills. The beneficiaries will be individual leaders, their organizations and, ultimately, the confederation we call the free enterprise system.

For further information, as the old saying goes, inquire within.

—Norman R. Augustine
Vice Chairman and Chief Executive Officer
Martin Marietta Corporation

1

LEADING

twenty fundamentals to remember

A leader is a man who has the ability to get other people to do what they don't want to do, and like it.

—Harry S. Truman

Leadership and learning are indispensable to each other.

—John F. Kennedy

There are twenty key fundamentals that form the basis for my approach to leadership. While some of these fundamentals will be discussed in greater detail later in this book, they are presented here to help the reader understand the foundations of my thinking on leadership of large organizations.

1. Trust Is Vital.

If you lead a large organization, it is essential that you be able to trust your subordinate leaders. Such trust is difficult for some leaders who want to direct every aspect of their organization. These leaders cannot find their way clear to trust people and, as a result, they do not nurture subleaders or give them the opportunity to exercise their full creative talents. To be a truly effective leader, particularly of a large organization, requires a great deal of trust in one's subordinates. This trust needs to be balanced with a willingness to remove people who cannot be trusted, and to make some tough decisions. Without trust and mutual respect among leaders and subordinate leaders, a large organization will often suffer a combination of low performance and poor morale. In the words of Frank Crane, ''You may be deceived if you trust too much, but you will live in torment if you do not trust enough."

2. *A Leader Should be a Good Teacher and Communicator.*

Teachership and leadership go hand-in-glove. The leader must be willing to teach skills, to share insights and experiences, and to work very closely with people to help them mature and be creative. In order to be a good teacher, a leader has to be a good communicator, and must be well organized and a goal-setter. By teaching, leaders can inspire, motivate, and influence subordinates at various levels.

If a leader is a good writer, communications, both up and down the organizational structure, will occur in a way that is meaningful, understandable, and has impact. If a good editor, the leader can work on papers, issues, and problems that come in written form to make sure they are clearly and simply stated so that they can have the maximum positive impact. If a good speaker, the leader can "reach out," making people feel good about themselves and take pride in their work. If a good listener, the leader can accept ideas, criticism, and other feedback that can improve the organization and create an atmosphere of excellence and caring. In the words of an unknown sage, "I never learned anything while I was talking." A dynamic communicator can motivate people to want to go back to work, committed to doing an even better job than they did in the past.

3. *A Leader Should Rarely Be a Problem Solver.*

A leader should facilitate problem solving, but should let subordinates solve most problems. The psychic reward that a subordinate gets from actually solving problems is quite important. It builds self-esteem and enhances the subordinate's ability to do still better in subsequent situations. Even though the leader can often solve the problem more quickly than subordinates, it is poor practice to be the problem solver. There are, of course, occasional exceptions to this rule. At times when the organization is in serious trouble, when subordinates appear unable to formulate a good answer to a problem, when only the leader has the expertise, the understanding, or the contacts to make the right decisions, the leader should step in. By being the problem solver of last resort, the leader can help the organization grow and thrive. General George Patton advised: "Never tell people how to do things. Tell them what to do and they will surprise you with their ingenuity."

4. A Leader Must Have Stamina.

The demands of big leadership are very heavy and no matter how well an executive may plan his or her daily, weekly, and monthly schedule there will be times when the pressures and demands will be onerous. Even though they may be very tired, leaders must be able to reach within themselves to find the reservoir of energy and creativity to handle crisis situations and other tough decisions. An intellectual and physical fitness program can help the executive be prepared for these difficult periods.

5. A Leader Must Manage Time Well and Use it Effectively.

One of the great faults of American executives is their general failure to discipline their schedules, their "in-boxes," their telephones, their travel schedules, and their meetings. Unlike many of their European and East Asian counterparts, American executives are often caught up in "activity traps" that fill up their day, keep them very busy, and allow little time for thoughtful reflection and strategic planning. Staying busy and working very long hours are not necessarily a measurement of leadership effectiveness. This strong carryover from our American cultural heritage of the Protestant ethic can be quite dysfunctional for top executives. Executives can control their schedules, at least in part, and there are many techniques and skills that can help them do so.

6. A Leader Must Have Technical Competence.

Executives must understand their businesses so that, as they carry out day-to-day activities, they know what they are doing. Leaders must not only understand the major elements of the businesses that they head, but also must keep up with the changes. If the leader has a high level of technical competence, then he or she should be able to trust his or her intuition. This combination of competence and intuition can be extremely powerful tools for a leader. Leaders probably would not have reached their present positions unless they had good intuition. They should continue to trust that intuition. Are they satisfied with the decisions they have made? Are the decisions others have made acceptable? Does something seem wrong? These are the kinds of questions that they should ask themselves. If their intuition sends them signals that would indicate the organization may be going in the wrong direction, they should respond, raise some additional questions, and postpone important decisions until they are reasonably comfortable that they are choosing the right course. To quote Ralph Waldo Emerson: "The essence of genius is spontaneity and instinct. Trust thyself." Part of intuition is having your "antennae" out, keeping your hand on the pulse of the organization, and being "street-smart" and "in touch." If something smells bad, take another look.

7. Leaders Must Not Condone Incompetence.

Leaders must be willing to set standards, to abide by those standards unwaveringly, and to require their subordinates to live by those standards. The leader is responsible for ensuring that the mission is accomplished. Inhibitors to this task, such as the continued presence of ineffective subordinates, drain the organization and its capable leaders of the time, energy, and attention needed to accomplish the mission. In such circumstances, leaders have a responsibility to the organization to remove those who stand in the way of success. Leaders are not serving themselves well; they're not serving the institution well; and, in many cases, they're not serving the incompetent individuals well by keeping them on in responsible positions. When it is necessary to remove people from key positions, leaders should meet with those individuals personally. The removal should be done with grace and style, but also with firmness. When you call individuals in to ask them to move on, you should be willing to do so—and not end the meeting unable to get to the point. See Chapter 5.

8. *Leaders Must Take Care of Their People.*

They should recognize not just the top performers but also the many others who are doing their jobs well, with good attitudes and a strong commitment to institutional goals. Leaders should *never* ask subordinates to write their own personal evaluations or effectiveness reports; leaders should write their effectiveness reports or their personal evaluations and make sure that these are done with care and style. Leaders should get up in the morning thanking people; at noontime they should thank more people; before going home at night, they should thank still more. Thanking people is an important part of taking care of them because it's taking care of their psychological health. Leaders should mentor outstanding subordinates while avoiding the pitfalls of cronyism. They should follow Pierce Chapron's advice when he helps people: "He who receives a benefit should never forget it; he who bestows should never remember it."

9. *Leaders Must Provide Vision.*

Leaders who are not planners are simply caretakers, gatekeepers and time-servers. Though they may run efficient and effective organizations, they do not really serve the long-term interests of the institution unless they plan, set goals, and provide strategic vision. Leaders who care about their missions and about their people normally want to leave their organizations in better shape and with a clearer strategic direction than when they took over. Good planning, goal-setting, and priority-setting can accomplish these things and create a marvelous legacy. Those leaders who are not visionaries, and many are not, should ensure that they have frequent contact with people who have a talent and an inclination for long-range planning, visionary thinking and innovation. The best leaders are agents for change and one of the best ways to ensure that this change is accomplished systematically is through good long-range planning. See Chapter 15.

10. Leaders Must Subordinate Their Ambitions and Egos to the Goals of the Unit or the Institution that They Lead.

Often leaders have to subvert their strong personal ambition in order to ensure that the development and maturation of their organizations and the movement towards higher standards of excellence and performance are accomplished in a careful and systematic way. The selfless leader gains the respect of subordinates and the support of superiors. Leaders must be willing to say "I was wrong," "I made a mistake," "I accept responsibility for our failure and am willing to accept the *full* consequences of that failure." If leaders are too ambitious for the organization, or too ambitious for themselves, they may drive the organization in dysfunctional directions. They may, in fact, become a part of the problem rather than a part of the solution.

11. Leaders Must Know How to Run Meetings.

Much of a leader's time is spent in meetings. Leaders should know what kind of meetings they're attending; they should establish the ground rules for the meetings; they should be actively involved in the meetings to make sure they stay on track; they should give individuals ample opportunity to express their views and their disagreements. Finally, leaders should know how to wrap up meetings, to draw conclusions, to set up the time and agenda for the next meeting on the subject, and to direct individuals in the meeting to carry out certain tasks as a result of the decisions that have been made. Leaders also must discontinue regular (weekly, monthly, quarterly) meetings that are not serving an important purpose. American leaders especially must fight the cultural tendency to hold long, undisciplined meetings with little useful output.

12. A Leader Must Be a Motivator.

Leaders must not only know how to motivate in general, but they also should teach their subordinate leaders so that they, in turn, will be strong in motivational skills. No leaders of large organizations can reach all their people on a regular basis, so they must count on subordinate leaders to provide much of the motivation. Commitment to mission, love of the job and the people, dedication to high standards, frequent reinforcement of the organization's plans and goals, strong incentive and reward programs, and lots of compliments for hard work and high performance, are all parts of the vital motivation factor.

13. *Leaders Must Be Visible and Approachable.*

In large organizations, the four-hour rule is a useful guide: leaders should spend no more than four hours a day in their offices. The rest of the time they should be out with their people, conducting meetings, and visiting subordinates in their work areas. They should be talking to lower level officials and getting their feedback on problem areas. They should be patting people on the back. They should be making short speeches. They should be handing out awards. They should be traveling widely throughout their organizations. They should be making contact with sister organizations and organizations at higher levels so they can ensure that important relationships are enhanced and problem areas identified early. When they are having meetings or discussions in their offices, they should never sit behind their desks, but should go to a couch or sofa—getting away from an imposing position which is often intimidating to subordinates. To make visitors feel comfortable, leaders should sit in the more sociable areas of their offices, close the door, and make the individual understand that nothing else matters except the subject that he or she has brought to the leader.

Another aspect of being approachable is getting involved in sports, hobbies, little theater groups, social gatherings, religious activities, etc. In this way, leaders can be out with subordinates, having contact with them at various levels. If, for instance, a leader jogs with subordinates, all kinds of interesting things that are going on in an organization may be discovered. A lower level subordinate usually will be more frank on a jogging trail than in an office. Company or unit softball leagues, basketball programs, tennis matches, or volleyball competitions serve the same purpose. A leader often can find out more about what's going on in a sporting or social atmosphere than in the front office. People will feel more comfortable if they see their leader in all kinds of different contexts: social, athletic, business, religious, personal, and so forth. Be benignly visible; be approachably visible. Some people are very visible but not approachable. One caution in this regard is appropriate: a "just-one-of-the-guys" kind of person is normally not a good leader. A leader must be special while being approachable.

14. Leaders Should Have a Sense of Humor.

Most of the time, leaders should laugh at themselves rather than at others. They should generally be willing to tell jokes or even embarrassing stories about their own mistakes to let people know that they are human, that they err, and that they are willing to admit errors. They should let people know that life is not so important that you can't sit back occasionally and be amused by what's happening. Humor can be a great reliever of tension; a story or a joke at times of crisis or difficulty can be very therapeutic. Be relaxed, be humorous with people, but don't use humor against people. Humor, delivered with an acid tongue and aimed at subordinates, can be very counterproductive. Off-color humor should be avoided since it diminishes the dignity of the leader and the organization. In addition, a leader should avoid treating *everything* as an occasion for humor. The "hail fellow well met" individuals are unlikely to get the respect they need to be effective executives.

15. Leaders Must Be Decisive, But Patiently Decisive.

Leaders should listen to all sides before deciding. They should, on occasion, postpone an important decision for a day or two, or even a week or two, while collecting additional information. However, a leader must be decisive. Institutions and organizations need decisions. Yet, they need a leader who is patiently decisive, who doesn't jump as soon as the first individual comes in and makes a recommendation for a decision. A leader should always look for contrasting views. If at all possible, he or she ought to sleep on important issues. Leaders should talk to their executive officers, deputies, spouses, or other people who can be trusted to forgo personal or parochial interests. A leader also should talk to people who may not like the tentative decision to find out what their opposing views might be. However, postponing the decision for many weeks or months is rarely the answer. A non-decision is itself a decision and should be recognized for what it is. Risk-taking is frequently an essential and healthy aspect of decisionmaking.

Leaders also must understand how to implement decisions. Decisions made are of little value if they are not implemented, so leaders must know how to develop implementing strategies. They must have follow-up systems to ensure that decisions are not only carried out, but carried out faithfully, in both substance and spirit.

16. Leaders Should Be Introspective.

Leaders should be able to look at themselves objectively and analyze where they have made mistakes, where they've turned people off and where they've headed down the wrong path. They must be able to look in the mirror and determine what they did right today, what they did wrong today, what decisions they need to go back to again, and how approachable they were. They should ask themselves if they have been too cooped up, too narrow, or too rigid. Introspection can be followed to a fault, however. Hamlets make poor leaders.

17. Leaders Should Be Reliable.

A leader should be careful about what commitments are made, but once those commitments are firm, nothing short of major health problems or a very serious crisis in business, institution, or family matters should alter them. Reliability is something that leaders must have in order to provide stability and strength to organizations. Important aspects of reliability are persistence and consistency. Leaders must be willing to be flexible, but consistency and coherence are important elements of large organizations and deserve the support of top leaders.

18. Leaders Should be Open-Minded.

The best leaders are the ones whose minds are never closed, who are interested in hearing new points of view, and who are eager to deal with new issues. Even after a decision has been made, a leader should be willing to listen to contrary views and

new approaches. Leaders shouldn't change their minds too frequently after a major decision has been made, but if they never
reconsider, they are beginning to show a degree of rigidity and
inflexibility that can spell trouble for the organization.

19. Leaders Should Establish and Maintain High Standards of Dignity.

When standards of dignity are established and emphasized, everyone can take pride in both the accomplishments and the
style of the operation. The leader's role is multifaceted. By
dressing well, being well mannered, avoiding profanity, helping subordinates through personal or family crises, conducting
ceremonies with dignity, welcoming newcomers with warmly
written personal letters, etc., leaders can accomplish a great
deal. A happy combination of substance and style leads to high
performance and morale.

20. Leaders Should Exude Integrity.

Leaders should not only talk about integrity, they must also operate at a high level of integrity. They should emphasize both
personal and institutional integrity. They should take corrective action when there are violations of integrity and upgrade
the standards of institutional integrity over time. A leader
should also ensure that everybody understands the leader's fundamental commitment to the values of their institution. Soon
after taking over a leadership position, a leader should look for
ways to demonstrate this commitment to integrity. Institutional
integrity cannot lie dormant until a crisis occurs; integrity must
be ingrained and must be supported by the leader and the organizational community. Of all the qualities a leader must have,
integrity is the most important.

2

TAKING OVER
the vital nature of the transition

When ever you are asked if you can do a job, tell em, 'Certainly I can!' Then get busy and find out how to do it.

—*Theodore Roosevelt*

Well begun is half done.

—*Horace*

Many individuals taking over executive positions fail to think through the transition process. They fail to plan to take charge, and so fail to maximize their opportunities to be well prepared for their new leadership responsibilities. By approaching the transition process in a systematic way and following a checklist carefully, a leader can be much more effective in the first few important weeks after taking over. The transition process is particularly important for someone coming into a large or complex organization.

An executive about to take over a large organization must deal with the problem of psychological transition, especially if he or she has never run a large organization before. This book will help you become a "big" leader by helping you think through the transition to leadership of large organizations.

One of the first things a new leader might do is to ask the present leader to make a tape recording outlining major issues, concerns, problems and frustrations that have occurred in the organization. On this tape, the departing leader should also discuss the personalities within the organization, with considerable emphasis on immediate subordinates. A frank evaluation of the major personnel problems that exist, and a candid analysis of people who need counselling and people who probably should be reassigned, also should be included. Additionally, the incumbent should outline in that tape any "skeletons in the closet" that exist in the organization so that the new leader can be sensitive to issues and problems that might not be visible during the crucial first few months. A caution here is in order: the new leader should not accept the information on the tape uncritically. He or she should evaluate the credibility and impartiality of the previous leader when listening to the tape.

Some new leaders prefer not to get an evaluation from the departing leader on the various strengths and weaknesses of subordinates in order to give subordinates a clean slate. I disagree with this approach because a new leader can make some major mistakes that can do great harm to the organization if he or she plays the game with a partial deck of cards. A new leader's knowledge of the strengths and weaknesses of key personnel should be as complete as possible.

If possible, the new leader should be permitted to have a few weeks before assuming new responsibilities to ask a number of transition questions. These questions should be answered (preferably in writing but, if not, orally) by the present leader, by the deputy, or by some key individuals within the organization. The most important questions to ask are: What is the mission, role, or desired output of the organization? What is the strategic plan? Financial situation? What are the dividend policies? What goals have been established? What are the established priorities? What is the current state of morale? Here it would be advisable to review the organization's most recent evaluation report to see what steps have been taken to correct deficiencies.

It is very common for organizations to lose sight of the desired output as leaders get caught up in solving day-to-day problems; yet, the output (or mission) must remain the first and foremost concern of the leader.

There are a variety of other questions which the new leader should ask before taking over the job. Many of these are outlined in the transition checklist in Appendix A, and some are discussed below.

What are the various means of communication that you have available to interact creatively with your subordinates? In many large organizations there are newspapers or newsletters published on a regular basis that will give you the opportunity to write a column outlining a subject that you want to share with your subordinates. Local radio or television is a marvelous way to reach the members of your team and their families. Staff meetings, trips to subordinate organizations, and speeches to various groups are just a few of the ways an active leader can reach out and communicate.

Who will report directly to you and how large is your span of control? A careful reading of the personnel records ahead of time as well as discussions with your predecessor and your superior can help you assess their qualifications. The personnel or human resources director in a large organization will be an important source of information.

What constituencies will you be serving, either directly or indirectly? Leaders of large organizations normally have to serve many constituencies, including their subordinates and their families, the retired community, interest groups, alumni, etc. It is useful to find out whom to meet with and who best represents the interests of these constituencies.

Who is your immediate boss and what are his or her leadership and management styles? Before taking charge, you should meet with your boss and get an evaluation of your new job as well as an understanding of your superior's satisfactions and dissatisfactions with the organization you are about to lead. If your boss feels the organization that you are about to head is in bad shape, you may wish to attempt to reach an understanding about how long it should take to get it back into shape. This discussion can lead to some very useful insights both about the organization and about your boss and his or her understanding of the problems of organizational rejuvenation. You should also meet with the key staff directors who work for your boss to get their views of problem areas and strengths within your new organization.

Are you responsible for geographically separated organizations? Do they report directly or indirectly to you? Most large organizations have geographically separated plants, divisions, or units that report to the top leader either directly or indirectly. It is easy for the leader to get caught up in a combination of corporate business at headquarters and in various outreach responsibilities, neglecting field operations. A general rule to follow is to spend a disproportionate amount of time with field organizations to demonstrate your concern, interest, and respect, as well as to update these organizations on your concerns and your changes in policy and plans.

What is the standard of integrity in the organization? Without constant nurturing, high standards of ethics can rapidly deteriorate as one breach of institutional standards quickly leads to another. The leader should review the reporting and inspection systems to ensure that they reinforce rather than undermine integrity.

What are the various standards of discipline? It is reasonably easy to ascertain whether deadlines are being met, if the products being produced are of high quality, and if overall performance is meeting acceptable standards. The leader should look carefully at the performance record of subordinate organizations and staff agencies to ensure that standards are being met and, when they are not, that prompt, appropriate action is taken.

What documents should you read and in what order? Plans, policy statements, and organizational histories (if available) are fine places to start your reading program. Your deputy or executive vice president should help prepare this list of documents for you. He or she should prioritize these documents so you can read the most important ones first.

Is there anything that, if made public, could embarrass my predecessor, the organization, or me? In other words, are there "skeletons" and, if so, in what closet? It is important to ascertain if there are key individuals in the organization who have serious health problems, including alcoholism, drug abuse, and psychiatric difficulties. In addition, it is useful to root out institutional "skeletons in the closet" that may not have been revealed in normal reporting for fear that the organization or the boss would look bad, or that corporate profits would suffer.

What is the overall size of the organization you are about to lead? Is the present organizational structure effective, and is it, at the same time, encouraging initiative and innovation? The new leader needs to dig into issues of organizational effectiveness to ensure that there is a workable span of control without too many people reporting directly to the leader.

It also is useful to find out if subordinate leaders have regular counselling sessions with their subordinates, and if poor performance is being identified and corrected. Additionally, the leader should look at the continuity of the organization for the next few years so that scheduled retirements and other departures of key subordinates can be identified and replacements recruited well in advance of departure dates. In addition, younger officials will look to you to establish a promotion system that will give them opportunities for upward mobility.

It is always useful to take an objective look at the individual that you are replacing. If the organization is in great shape and your predecessor has been a popular leader, it may be worthwhile to continue past policies, to let everybody know that you are honored to follow someone of such stature, and to articulate your hope that you will be able to keep the unit's performance and morale at its high level. If the individual was very popular, but the performance of the organization has been fairly low, you have a greater challenge. You must be willing to demand higher performance levels without denigrating the leader you replace. If you are following an individual who was very cold, harsh, or unpopular, but the organization has been performing well, then your task is easy. By reaching out to people, by thanking and complimenting them often, and by being approachable, you can lift performance even higher by enhancing morale. Finally, if you take over an organization that is performing badly, you can take the approach that it is time for everyone in the organization to chart a new course, to recognize the deficiencies of past performances, and to work together to upgrade performance levels across the entire organization.

Two common problems with decisionmaking should be discussed with subordinates during the initial phases of the transition process: the "Oh, by the way" problem and the "nonconcurrence through silence" issue. By discussing these issues with your key staff personnel and your subordinate leaders, you can help them understand some important ground rules with regard to the decisionmaking process under your leadership.

The "Oh, by the way" problem is a common phenomenon in most large organizations. At the end of a scheduled meeting, the leader will sometimes be approached by a subordinate who will say, "Oh, by the way, I would like to raise a new issue and get your decision." Immediately, you should be cautious, since often the issue requires coordination, and a quick decision by you can be a mistake. A useful way to handle this situation is to listen carefully, to ask the individual to coordinate the issue with other staff and field agencies, and to decline the opportunity to make a decision (or even a tentative decision) prior to the completion of the coordination process. Sometimes this requires extraordinary self-discipline on the part of the leader since the subordinate may be pushing hard for a quick decision—there may be some urgency involved—and the leader may not want to appear indecisive. However, in many cases, a quick decision is a bad idea and will come back to haunt the leader.

One ground rule that may be worth establishing is having subordinates raise the "Oh, by the ways" *before* scheduled staff meetings rather than after them. In this way the executive may choose to discuss the issue in the meeting with key subordinates present, or, if this issue is important or urgent enough, to call a special meeting immediately following the scheduled meeting. Of course, "Oh, by the ways" can come up at almost anytime—at lunch, on the tennis court, at the bar, on a trip, etc. The leader should be receptive to new ideas but should be very careful about quick decisions. For instance, even a reply like, "That sounds OK in principle" might cause an aggressive subordinate to race off and do something that may cause your organization great grief.

Leaders may wish to establish a "no nonconcurrence through silence" rule. Subordinates who do not concur with the decisions being made in meetings and discussions must understand that they have a responsibility to speak up. By remaining silent during these discussions, they do the leader a grave disservice. A major part of subordinates' duties is to speak out on issues, particularly when they disagree with either the context or the thrust of the discussion in which a decision is being made. The leader must create a decisionmaking environment in which subordinates feel free to express concerns, raise new options, and disagree with the leader and others. One useful way to draw out comments from the more introverted subordinates prior to making a decision on an issue under discussion is to ask, by name, the views of specific individuals in the meeting who have not spoken up during the discussion.

Leaders must work hard to avoid "group-think"—a situation in which there is too much compatibility and a consensus on issues is arrived at too quickly. False consensus, excessive conformity, and group-think are not in the interest of any large organization. Even though the concerns raised by subordinates may be parochial or ill-considered, the leader must be willing to listen carefully to these concerns before a final decision is made. There is a direct relationship between the thoroughness and openness of the decisionmaking process and the effectiveness of the implementation process. If subordinates are given a full opportunity to express their views prior to the making of the decision, they will be more willing to carry out the decision after it is made, even though the decision may not be the one that the subordinate would have chosen.

Leaders who have gone through the transition process carefully and systematically and know what they want to do, when they want to do it, how they want to make decisions, and how they want to approach issues, can quickly get the attention and respect of their people and can make a big difference in both the future performance and self-esteem of the unit. If the new leader also creates an atmosphere that encourages high integrity, planning, and creativity, the organization can soon become the model for others to emulate.

Having addressed all these questions, the new leader should assess the performance of the organization and its ability to accomplish its mission. Your boss and his or her key staff directors can be very helpful, and considerable time should be spent reading the reports of and talking to auditors, inspectors, and evaluators. It is quite common to find an organization having an inflated view of its own level of performance. Although more unusual, there are organizations which, at times, have a deflated view of themselves; therefore, it is important for the new leader to walk into this job with an objective understanding of both the perceptions and the realities. Thorough assessment is vital. By establishing goals early and articulating those goals in a way that can be easily understood by subordinates, a leader can quickly establish agendas, priorities, and objectives. For the conscientious leader, this process never ends.

After the leader has been in charge for two or three months, he or she should write a philosophy letter. Using his or her own words, the leader should state the goals and priorities of the organization and the particular points of emphasis that are important to the leader. This letter can serve many useful purposes. It can let everyone know that the new boss is in charge, has a good grasp of the organization, has established clear and understandable goals, and has laid out areas of emphasis.

The letter, in draft form, should be circulated among key subordinates for comments and criticism. It is important that these subordinates be comfortable with the letter since they will be responsible for supporting both the goals and the underlying philosophy. The contents of the letter should be summarized in the company, university, or post newspaper; in addition, the letter itself should be widely circulated. It should be given to all perspective new employees so that they can, at an early date, identify with both the organization and the leader.

Specific points that may be useful to outline in the philosophy letter include: the rich and successful history of the organization, the commitment of the organization to specific goals and community goals, the need for high personal and institutional integrity, the strategic vision of the leader and the organization, the policy of decentralization and empowerment of subordinate leaders, the need for innovation, and the process whereby creative ideas move up in the organization.

The letter should be brief (no more than five pages), upbeat, and nonthreatening, and it should clearly reflect the thoughts and dreams of the leader. By forcing themselves to write this letter within three months of taking over, leaders make the important psychological leap from being the new boss to being the person fully in charge. After leaders have been in charge for about a year, they should review the letter and revise and rewrite it as necessary to reflect any changes in their vision, goals, and philosophy of leadership.

3

HIRING

the right people for the right jobs

Recipe for success: First, make a reputation for creative genius. Second, surround yourself with partners who are better than you are. Third, leave them to get on with it.

—David Ogilvey

Mistrust a subordinate who never finds fault with his superior.

—John C. Collins

One of the more important responsibilities of the leader of a large organization is hiring immediate subordinates and other key people in the organization. Personnel records and resumés are useful starting points in identifying those individuals who are clearly strong candidates for the position under consideration. However, additional research needs to be done. Contact individuals who know the prospective candidate. It is particularly useful to talk to people who have been the individual's supervisors in recent years to get candid evaluations of the performance of the individual in other job situations. All this research is well worth doing to ensure the selection process is as complete and objective as possible. However, in many cases, this research is not enough and an interview is necessary.

The interview should be conducted systematically; a checklist should be used (although the checklist should be in the leader's head rather than on paper, in order to increase the informality of the interview process), and key questions should be asked. See Appendix A (Checklist 3).

Do you want this job and why?   This should be the first question asked of a prospective key subordinate. If the candidate is not really interested in the job, has serious reservations about the job, or has motivations for the job you don't find useful or particularly attractive, the interview can be wrapped up quickly, and the individual eliminated from consideration. In the following discussion, there are a number of additional questions. These can be asked in any order.

Why should I hire you? What are your strengths and what are your weaknesses?   These questions sometimes set an interviewee back a bit, but it is very useful to find out how introspective the individual is. If the individual lists a large number of strengths and no weaknesses or vice versa, you may have identified an individual who will not serve you well. An individual who not only outlines individual strengths but is aware of and working on weaknesses is an individual who probably deserves very serious consideration. Those people who are self-assured to the point of arrogance or who lack self-confidence are not likely to be major contributors to your organization.

What are the best books and professional journals that you have read in recent years; why do you consider them so good; what insights did these readings give you?   This is a good way to find out how well-read an individual is—how intellectually curious, how open to ideas, suggestions, and insights that good books can provide, and how well this person is keeping up with his or her discipline or profession. It has been my experience that people who are not widely read and who do not have the intellectual curiosity or the interest to read professional journals and books that help them improve are basically self-limited. They are not likely to grow and to make major contributions beyond the level of their present competence. If you find a person who is well-read, you can probably gain some interesting and useful insights about the individual and you can have a discussion that will be a learning experience on both sides. The best leaders often are the ones who are intellectually curious.

What is your leadership philosophy and style? This is a good way to ascertain whether the individual knows how to operate efficiently, knows what subordinates feel, knows how to set goals and priorities, and knows how to be introspective. Another question that is useful is, "If I were to ask your present subordinates how they would describe your leadership style, what would they say?" The answer can be insightful because it can quickly draw out the attitude that the individual has toward subordinates and whether the individual is willing to acknowledge the fact that there may be some subordinates who are uncomfortable with his or her personal style. The answer, in combination with what you might find out from other sources, can give you an understanding of how well this individual grasps the realities of his or her present situation.

If you are not selected for this position, who would you recommend? This is a useful question to find out how a person judges the job, the qualities that are needed for it, and how closely the applicant is in contact with other individuals with similar qualifications. It also will bring out how willing an individual is to acknowledge that there may be others who are as well, or better, qualified for this job.

Are there any ''skeletons in your closet''? This is a sensitive question and is best asked in a more considerate way, such as, "Are there any general health, family, psychiatric, or other problems that are worrying you that may cause you difficulties or prevent your full effectiveness in this job?" or "Is there anything that would be helpful for me to know now which might be an embarrassment if it surfaces later?" In any case, such a question needs to be asked to help determine how candid the individual is willing to be with you. You may want to hire the person regardless of his or her response, but it's useful to have all the cards on the table. If, in fact, important information is withheld from you that you find out from other sources, you will discover that this person is unwilling to be honest and candid with you.

What are your long-term personal goals? It's helpful to find out where an individual is heading in life. Does this person want to work for you forever or just want this job for a year or two? What are his or her goals after this? Is the applicant hyperambitious or ambitious in a positive way?

If you were in charge of this organization, what would you do? (This question, of course, is most appropriate for candidates who know the organization quite well.) This is a way to find out if candidates have original ideas and insights, and whether they have a willingness to speak up about aspects of the organization that they don't like or which make them uncomfortable. If, for instance, the candidate says nothing, you might want to ask yourself "Does this person have the ability to make significant changes where needed, or is this someone who will always be satisfied with the status quo?"

What is it that annoys you in your present organization? This is a question that you could ask someone who already works for you. It is also a useful question to ask individuals who do not yet work for you regarding another organization. You might be able to learn a great deal about their personalities. Also, they may reveal aspects about their interaction in an organizational framework that may reinforce your desire to hire them, or, conversely, give you indications that you would not be comfortable with them.

What are the standards of integrity in your present organization? This is a good way to lead into the integrity question. Do prospective employees have high standards of personal integrity? Do they set high standards of institutional integrity? Do they think or care much about integrity? This can lead to a useful discussion on the issues of institutional and personal ethics and the role that they play in an organizational framework.

Whom in your present organization do you respect the most and why? This question tends to highlight certain aspects of personality and background that may provide insights into what a candidate thinks are the important aspects of leadership. If a person admires a strong leader and knows why, as well as what leadership qualities he or she would like to emulate, you may have discovered an individual who has been seriously thinking about leadership and who may be the kind of person you would want to hire as one of your subordinate leaders.

What is the toughest problem you have faced in your career? How did you handle it? This question can be a useful way to determine how well the individual has been tested and what has been learned from a tough experience. It is one way to determine how introspective an individual is.

Since the hiring of immediate subordinates is important, it should not be delegated except in certain situations. If you, as the boss, have a trusted deputy who has great insights into the personalities of individuals, has had a lot of experience in interviewing people for jobs, has a good feeling for the organization and knows your particular desires and proclivities, delegating the hiring practice to your deputy makes good sense. It's also sometimes useful to draw together a search committee that may have expertise that you don't have and whose members would be capable of asking the most relevant questions. You can use this committee to screen out and reduce the list to a small number; but, ultimately, the leader must make the choice.

A leader should be actively involved in hiring those individuals who work directly for him. Subordinate leaders should normally be given the authority to hire their subordinates. If a big leader wishes to maintain veto authority over the hiring of key subordinates whom he or she will not supervise directly, this veto should be used with great care. The veto can help reduce cronyism on the part of subordinate leaders, but it should actually be used very seldom.

Finally, leaders should fully consider the subtle but important aspect of leader-subordinate relationships known commonly as "chemistry" when evaluating various candidates for a key position. The leader should consider the chemistry factor not only in subordinate-leader interactions but also in peer relationships among subordinates. This is one of the reasons that interviews are important; a set of personnel records cannot help very much in determining how well an individual will fit into the environment you have established in your organization.

One caution about "chemistry" is in order. In seeking subordinates with the right "chemistry," there is always the danger that prejudices and biases will creep in that the executive may not even be aware of. A leader should be careful not to use "bad chemistry" as an excuse for not hiring a well qualified candidate who is not of the same race or sex or does not come from the same cultural, social, or educational background as the leader. The top personnel officer must also be careful not to narrow the candidates down in order to satisfy the leader's hidden (or not-so-hidden) prejudices.

4

COUNSELLING SUBORDINATES

the value of one-on-ones

Encourage your staff to be candid with you. Ask their advice and listen to it. Top bananas have no monopoly on ideas.

—*David Ogilvey*

Many receive advice, only the wise profit from it.

—*Syrus*

A leader of an organization should have private sessions with immediate subordinates about once every six months to deal specifically with performance counselling. The purpose of these sessions is to trade ideas, insights, and suggestions, and to learn about the health of the organization. It is an opportunity for personal counselling, but, to an even greater extent, it is an opportunity for subordinates to talk quietly, off the record, with the boss in a meaningful way, to get things off their chests, and to suggest ideas and initiatives. Further, individual objectives for improvement can be set for review six months later. These sessions also give subordinates the feeling that their ideas really count and that the boss is interested in listening to them.

In observing leaders from many nations at various levels, it has been my experience that these one-on-one sessions are the exception rather than the rule. Although leaders talk about how they counsel their people, in actuality counselling sessions seldom take place. A quick meeting in the hall, a brief comment or two in a staff meeting, or a passing comment here and there are not counselling sessions.

A useful way to cover the important issues in a counselling session is to ask the following questions:

What aspects of this organization do you like the most? It is useful to start the session on a positive note. This question can be a useful "ice-breaker" since the subordinate may be a bit uncomfortable in the first few minutes in the front office with the boss.

What areas around here bother you the most? This question allows the subordinate to voice those areas of real heartburn. It might be that the subordinate does not like the job, the secretary, the work hours, the level of authority, the living conditions, the pay, or the amount of recognition received. It is a good opportunity to "smoke out" those things that really bother subordinates.

What are your ideas for improving this organization? This is an opportunity not only to get some ideas but also to find out where the "idea people" are. In every organization there are only a few people who actually have useful, innovative ideas. This question often helps identify the folks who really care about improving the organization and have ideas about how to do so.

What policies, procedures, tactics, subordinate organizations, systems, etc., should we divest ourselves of and on what kind of a schedule (now, next year, five years from now, etc.)? Here's a way to discover whether the individual has thought about the problem of what programs we ought to abandon, what things we are doing that inhibit the accomplishment of the organization's mission, what things were useful to do in the past but are no longer useful, and what kind of divestiture strategy we should develop.

In your judgment, who are the most innovative, helpful and cooperative people in this organization? "Who are the people who are not pulling their load?" is often an unfair question and one that people are reluctant to answer. If you ask them, "Who are the best people?" you'll not only find out who the best people are, but you'll also notice, over time, who is seldom or never mentioned. The ones who are never mentioned are normally the ones not pulling their load, not being cooperative, or who have some other problem. In most cases, you will know who the best people are already but, on occasion, you will be surprised. Someone who is particularly quiet, for instance, might be mentioned as an absolutely marvelous and contributing individual.

What are your personal goals while you are in this organization? This is a fine way to ascertain the goals, dreams, and aspirations of your subordinates. Some will prefer to stay at their present levels; others will want to move to another division or location; others will want to move upward. Answers to this question can be very helpful as the leader does personnel planning. Here you get an idea of an employee's long-range plans: Where (to what job) would you like to go next? Why? When would you like to go? What ambitions do you have? How happy are you here? Many insights about your people and organization surface as a result of these questions.

What do you consider to be your most significant weaknesses? Again, if the individual doesn't think any weaknesses exist, you may have a problem right there. In many cases, the individual may outline personal weaknesses fairly well, but may miss one or two areas. This gives you the opportunity to probe gently about a person's ability to write, to speak, to cooperate, to lead, to manage. You can also probe into other areas of possible weakness that may not have been identified. Although a delicate question, it often opens the door to excellent counselling opportunities.

What self-improvement programs do you have underway? Are you pursuing advanced education? Are you taking professional courses? Are you in a Toastmaster's Club to learn how to be a better speaker? Are you taking speed-reading courses? If the individual is doing nothing for self-improvement, you have an opportunity to highlight the value of self-improvement.

What do you think your chances are for promotion to the next level, and in what time frame? Here you get an opportunity to have individuals evaluate their own potential for promotion and for moving up to higher levels of responsibility. You will find out whether their expectations are inflated, as they are in some cases. If they do have inflated expectations and you are aware of weak or mediocre professional records, you can give them a candid appraisal. It is important that you be frank as well as factual so that individuals with poor performance records are not destroyed emotionally if they fail to be promoted at some later date.

What bothers you the most about my decisions and my leadership style? In what areas have my decisions or policies caused you to waste your time? Here's a great opportunity to find out a little bit about yourself. Answers to that question may include: "You're too intense"; "You're too hard on people"; "You've put too much emphasis in certain areas and not enough in others"; "What we are doing in a certain area is a waste of time and money." Some people, of course, will tell you that you're wonderful and not give you any indication of your problem areas, but the better, more mature subordinates will almost always say "Yes, there are a few areas; let me make a few suggestions."

What are the goals that you have established for your organization? Here you are asking subordinates what goals they have set for their own organizations. Do their goals conform to the goals you have established for the parent organization? Perhaps the individual has established goals that are more thoughtful or innovative than your own.

Please evaluate the performance of the organization, unit, or group that you led over the past six months. Please outline the high and low points of the period. This is a useful way to ascertain the objectivity of subordinate leaders when it comes to their own organizations.

The counselling checklist should not be read; it should be in your head. At the end of the counselling session, you have the responsibility not only to point out the strengths of the individual, but also to point out weaknesses. If you call in persons who are not doing particularly well and do not tell them so, you are not conducting honest, fair, and complete counselling sessions. Counselling takes a lot of time and is hard work. Sometimes the subordinate's reaction to criticism becomes very emotional, but counselling is something that needs to be scheduled regularly and done well. For each one-on-one session, you should allow one hour. Often the session may last only twenty or thirty minutes, but there may be a requirement to listen for a long time when serious problems surface. As a general rule, the session should start and end on positive notes. Even if the individual has not been performing well, a compliment at the end of the session is important.

Sometimes, your counselling session with a subordinate must concentrate wholly on his or her shortcomings or failures. These sessions are easy to avoid or postpone, but they must be done in a timely and tactful manner. If a subordinate makes a serious mistake that clearly requires corrective action, you should immediately have a private meeting. Public admonishment should be avoided, but private counselling should take place quickly and firmly and all important areas should be covered carefully and systematically. An excellent example of counselling of this type was Robert E. Lee's session with J.E.B. Stuart when he arrived at the Gettysburg battlefield two days late. The following comes from Michael Shaara's Pulitzer Prizewinning historical novel, *The Killer Angels,** my favorite book.

He saw a man coming toward him, easy gait, rolling and serene, instantly recognizable: Jeb Stuart. Lee stood up. This must be done. Stuart came up, saluted pleasantly, took off the plumed hat and bowed.

'You wish to see me, sir?'

'I asked to see you alone,' Lee said quietly. 'I wished to speak

*From *The Killer Angels* by Michael Shaara. Copyright © 1974 by Michael Shaara. Reprinted by permission of David McKay Co., a Division of Random House, Inc.

with you alone, away from other officers. That has not been possible until now. I am sorry to keep you up so late.'

'Sir, I was not asleep,' Stuart drawled, smiled, gave the sunny impression that sleep held no importance, none at all.

Lee thought: here's one with faith in himself. Must protect that. And yet, there's a lesson to be learned. He said, 'Are you aware, General, that there are officers on my staff who have requested your court-martial?'

Stuart froze. His mouth hung open. He shook his head once quickly, then cocked it to one side.

Lee said, 'I have not concurred. But it is the opinion of some excellent officers that you have let us all down.'

'General Lee,' Stuart was struggling. Lee thought: now there will be anger. 'Sir,' Stuart said tightly, 'if you will tell me who these gentlemen...'

'There will be none of that.' Lee's voice was cold and sharp. He spoke as you speak to a child, a small child, from a great height. 'There is no time for that.'

'I only ask that I be allowed—'

Lee cut him off. 'There is no time,' Lee said. He was not a man to speak this way to a brother officer, a fellow Virginian; he shocked Stuart to silence with the iciness of his voice. Stuart stood like a beggar, his hat in his hands.

'General Stuart,' Lee said slowly, 'you were the eyes of this army.' He paused.

Stuart said softly, a pathetic voice, 'General Lee, if you please . . .' But Lee went on.

'You were my eyes. Your mission was to screen this army from the enemy cavalry and to report any movement by the enemy's main body. That mission was not fulfilled.'

Stuart stood motionless.

Lee said, 'You left this army without word of your movements, or of the movements of the enemy, for several days. We were forced into battle without adequate knowledge of the enemy's position, or strength, without knowledge of the ground. It is only by God's grace that we have escaped disaster.'

'General Lee.' Stuart was in pain, and the old man felt pity, but this was necessary; it had to be done as a bad tooth has to be pulled, and there was no turning away. Yet even now he felt the pity rise, and he wanted to say, it's all right, boy, it's all right; this is only a lesson, just one painful quick moment of learning, over in a moment, hold on, it'll be all right. His voice began to soften. He could not help it.

'It is possible that you misunderstood my orders. It is possible I did not make myself clear. Yet this must be clear; you with your cavalry are the eyes of the army. Without your cavalry, we are blind, and that has happened once, but must never happen again.'

There was a moment of silence. It was done. Lee wanted to reassure him, but he waited, giving it time to sink in, to take effect, like medicine. Stuart stood breathing audibly. After a moment he reached down and unbuckled his sword, theatrically, and handed it over with high drama in his face. Lee grimaced, annoyed, put his hands behind his back, half turned his face. Stuart was saying that since he no longer held the General's trust, but Lee interrupted with acid vigor.

'I have told you that there is no time for that. There is a fight tomorrow, and we need you. We need every man, God knows. You must take what I have told you and learn from it as a man does. There has been a mistake. It will not happen again. I know your quality. You are a good soldier. You are as good a cavalry officer as I have known, and your service to this army has been invaluable. I have learned to rely on your information; all your reports are always accurate. But no report is useful if it does not reach us. And that is what I wanted you to know. Now.' He lifted a hand. 'Let us talk no more of this.'

Regular counselling has enormous value to a leader. I cannot emphasize too strongly how much I have gained as far as constructive criticism, new insights, and fresh ideas from these sessions. They are well worth the time of all executives and subordinates.

5

FIRING

the role of the leader

My wire was sent to get you to toughen up—to can these fellows who cannot produce. I want you to come out of this a real commander.

—*Letter from General Hap Arnold to
Lieutenant General Ira Eaker, Commander,
Eighth Air Force in England,
June 1943*

A leader must be able to look a man in the eye when he fires him and weep for him at the same time.

—*James Stockdale*

Leaders of organizations occasionally need to remove people for a number of reasons: to remove incompetents, to reinforce standards, to punish violations of integrity, etc. The leader normally should fire individuals himself and not delegate that task. If, however, a leader has a very large organization, some delegation may be necessary. In any case, people who work directly for the leader should be fired by the boss.

Before an individual is removed for any reason, it is the responsibility of the leader to call the individual in for counselling, to explain forthrightly the deficiency, and to let the individual know where his or her job performance has been substandard. If, after a period of a few months, the performance standards still do not reach an acceptable level, the leader should seriously consider removing the individual from the position he or she holds. If the leader chooses this course of action, he should meet with the individual and with firmness remove him or her of the position. One approach is to tell the individual that the leader has lost confidence in his or her ability to do that job. During this session it is important for the leader to give the individual who is being removed the opportunity to explain what problems exist and how he or she feels about this action; the leader should be a patient and passive listener. It is a very traumatic experience for an individual to be fired, for in most cases it will be the first time. The leader has a responsibility to help the employee work through this difficult experience. Let the employee know specifically that you're asking her or him to leave because you feel that it's your responsibility as a leader. It is also useful during this session to point out that now, in being removed, the employee might go through a difficult period in life, both personally, and with the family. You should talk at length to the individual about future prospects. If appropriate, offer to help in finding the employee a new position. You should explain that you will write a final effectiveness report or evaluation with care to ensure that the individual's strengths as well as weaknesses are outlined fairly.

One technique that I use which at times has been of some help in easing the pain of the subordinate is to explain that I was once fired from a key job. I discuss how this experience affected me and my family, the thoughts that went through my mind at the time it occurred and in the months that followed and the fact that the next job I was placed in was considered a poor one by my contemporaries. I explain that I learned a great deal from the experience and in the long term benefited from having experienced a major setback in my life, for I was able to move away from an impossible interpersonal situation with my boss to a place where I was welcome and where my talents were appreciated. I also explain that I was never told by my boss that I was being fired nor had I ever been counselled by him ahead of time.

There may be some cases in which the individual has failed so badly in performance, integrity, or some other area, that you must be quite tough on the final report. If the employee is being fired for cause (not just for substandard performance, but for a gross violation of integrity or extremely poor performance), there should be no question remaining in the subordinate's mind—or in the final report—about why he or she is being fired.

People often get fired because they are not doing a particular job well, but they still have talents and abilities that can be applied elsewhere. It is often your responsibility as a leader to ensure that such individuals are moved into positions where they will have the opportunity to use and exploit their talents.

In some cases it's appropriate for the leader to suggest early retirement or a very significant job change. If the individual has demonstrated a real weakness in personal ability to do very basic things within the organization, it is useful to be straightforward with the individual and suggest that retirement might be in order.

It might be helpful here to explain a few situations I have faced in having to remove individuals for specific reasons. When I was in charge of the National War College, there were thirty-five professors from various professional and academic backgrounds; some had tenure and others were there for three or four years. I had to remove a professor before the end of the academic year because I was getting bad feedback on his attitude, his teaching ability, and his failure to organize his courses properly. I called him in and told him it was time for him to move on and explained why. We were able to find him a job where he was clearly competent. Although he was bitter about his experiences at the College and was not pleased with me, I think the move was best for him, and certainly best for the College. If he had stayed at the College, there probably would have been further damage to his career as a result of his continuing failure to meet our expectations.

When I was running a large staff organization, I had to fire a man who was in charge of a division which consisted of ten professionals and two secretaries. He treated a group of talented and hardworking young people as if they were unreliable or immature or both. He moved on to another job which took advantage of his creativity and energy, but where he had no one to supervise directly. He performed well.

On another occasion I removed an Air Force colonel who was a base commander. He was in charge of about 800 individuals, including civil engineers, security police and many other people responsible for the combat support of a tactical fighter wing in Europe. This man was married and lived with his wife on base; he also had a girlfriend downtown. He was embarrassing himself, his family, and the Wing since it was widely known that his girlfriend had moved into a nearby apartment. I told him that I could not tolerate that kind of activity, especially in light of strictly established policies which he himself was responsible for enforcing.

Another example of note would be the alcoholic who worked for me when I was at an international military headquarters in Northern Germany. He was from a European nation. After some counselling by me and the senior officer from his country, I asked him to leave short of his normal tour of duty. It took a number of months before we could move him out because of the personnel system in his country. He was removed for chronic absenteeism and his unwillingness to face up to his problem and seek professional help.

A CEO of a major newspaper chain, who has been a good friend for thirty years, shared with me recently his most difficult experience in his over twenty years as a CEO. For many months, he had been hearing rumors of morale problems at one of his newspapers in a city many miles from the corporate headquarters. He had also received rumors, from both within his company and from old friends who lived in the city in question, that the general manager of the newspaper had made sexual advances toward a number of young men in that community. The general manager, a man in his 40's, had been with the firm since graduating from college more than twenty years before. He was a close friend of the CEO and had had a brilliant career working his way up from cub reporter to editor to general manager.

The CEO also learned that this general manager, who had never married, was drinking heavily and at a recent convention had made very open, blatant, and greatly unappreciated advances towards two young sons of another newspaperman.

The CEO called in the general manager and told him that for many reasons it was time for the two to part company. The CEO gave him a very generous departure package and told him that if anyone approached him for a recommendation on the general manager, he would recommend him, but with appropriate reservations.

The CEO fired an old friend and trusted employee because he publicly embarrassed a company that by its very nature was in the public eye constantly.

A CEO of a large research firm provided me with an interesting insight about employees with splendid educational credentials and highly developed technical skills. He has found that most employees who are not performing up to standards are the first to realize it. In addition, he feels it normally takes him about three months to learn of the poor performance. By that time the employees usually know they are in trouble. The top executive then counsels them and gives them about six months to raise the performance level appreciably. If the employee realizes, in the next few months, that he or she will not be able to reach levels of expected performance, that individual has often already worked out some alternative plans for the next job. Hence the departure interview can usually be accomplished without hard feelings and loss of friendship.

There are a number of subtleties to be considered when the leader makes the decision to remove a subordinate from a position. There is a continuum of choices between a "hard" firing and a "soft" firing, and the leader should think through the various options quite carefully. Leaders should seek advice from their deputies, their lawyers, and their personnel directors (and, on occasion, from their expert on public relations, their psychiatrist, or their chaplain). Before the individual who is to be removed from office is called in, the leader must fully understand what authority is available, what the legal implications may be, how easy it will be to find a suitable replacement, etc. Consideration of the impact on the performance and morale of the organization which may result from this action may also be in order.

Leaders who never fire anyone may be doing a disservice

to their institution; as a result, many other people take advantage of the fact that they are safe from the real discipline of being removed from their positions. Therefore, a deserved firing is not only the right thing to do, but it also sets the tone to let people know that there are certain standards of performance and ethics to be met. It is an important part of any leader's responsibility to fire individuals who, *after proper counselling,* fail to live up to these standards.

6

LEADING IN CRISES

coolness and flexibility

The Chinese use two brush strokes to write the word 'crisis.' One brush stroke stands for danger, the other for opportunity. In a crisis, be aware of the danger—but recognize the opportunity.

—Richard M. Nixon

The only way I know to handle failure is to gain historical perspective, to think about men who have successfully lived with failure in our religious and classical past.

—James Stockdale

In the high-pressure world that all of us live in, it is not just the mayors of major cities, police and fire department chiefs, hospital emergency room staff, and military leaders who have to deal with crisis situations. Business leaders must be prepared for such diverse crises as the poisoning of drugs (the Tylenol crisis of the mid-1980s being just one example), the leakage of nuclear radiation or poisonous gases (the Three Mile Island nuclear incident and the Bhopal gas leak disaster in India come to mind), hostile corporate takeover attempts, stock market crashes, etc. Although my personal experiences with crises have dealt largely with international incidents and war, many principles and rules of thumb apply quite nicely to crises across the spectrum of business, nonprofit, and military activities.

No matter how well a leader plans, anticipates problems, and reacts in normal day-to-day activity, crises will occur. The enormity of a crisis, the time constraints, the fact that people's lives may be in danger, or other unique factors will present challenges that will test a leader severely and call upon skills and leadership techniques not normally tested. Individuals who face a crisis should be aware that they will often be short on facts, emotions may be running high, and the "fog of war" will lead to much confusion. Even though all the options may not be ideal, the leader must be decisive.

Four major aspects of crisis leadership are flexibility, innovation, simplicity, and empowerment (of subordinates). The leader must be willing to show flexibility, be open to suggestions on how to solve crises, and be willing to allow emergent leaders to come forward to assist. A hallmark of crisis leadership is keeping things simple—asking people to do things that they are already trained to do, and not asking them to do new things with which they are unfamiliar.

Some executives deal with crises on almost a day-to-day basis. A principal of a very large, racially and ethnically diverse high school in a suburban area near a large city shared with me many of the difficulties he has faced in recent years: suicides, attempted suicides, gang fights, severe drug incidents, homosexual activity between teachers and students, attempted rapes, etc. Executives in these kinds of situations need to plan carefully in anticipation of upcoming problems. Crisis response teams should be formed and ready. Quick access to police and fire departments as well as to nearby hospitals needs to be worked out in advance. Principals need to reach out to these agencies so the officials there will be responsive to their needs, particularly in times of crisis. The principal and his or her vice principals need to be very visible and very approachable so that they can be alerted ahead of time to upcoming problems. Through quick action they can head off many crises and handle speedily the ones that do develop.

One technique that this principal uses when he hears of upcoming trouble might be labelled preemptive warning. He starts spreading the word with tuned in students (students who are basically supportive of school policies but who are also in close personal contact with students who may plan activities that would be disruptive or destructive to good order and discipline) that he is aware of what is about to happen and will pass out severe punishment if it is carried out. He puts the word out on what the punishment will be and if the act takes place he passes out the punishment as he has previously advertised. This gives him a lot of credibility at a time of great tension and often stops the activity from ever taking place. He also uses the language of the corridor to get his message across. Without using profanity, he uses such terms as "If you do this, you are history," or, "You do this and it's the highway." He is not afraid to demonstrate his strong emotional commitment to his school and his standards. Since his students are committed to his school and his program, his tough words and emotional commitment have real impact, especially at times of high tension. His presence in the corridors and at all the major sporting events provides not only support for student activities but also a deterrent to disruptive or violent behavior. A leader must be more than a good crisis manager: he or she should anticipate and head off crises.

In many acute crises, such as natural disasters, fires, and industrial explosions, as well as in crises normally associated with the military, such as terrorist acts, low-intensity conflict, and war, the leader may not have the communications on hand to be able to manage them. Additionally, the leader may be isolated from the crisis (e.g., be taken a hostage), be hurt or injured, have had a heart attack, or for other reasons have been incapacitated. In anticipation of facing crises, the leader must identify and train other leaders who can pick up the ball and handle the situation.

The individual who is involved in handling a crisis must be technically competent and must understand the people, the organization, the mission, the goals, and the priorities. A leader in a peacetime crisis—as well as leaders in combat—cannot operate with only a superficial knowledge of what the organization is about and what its capabilities are. The leader in a crisis situation also must be dispassionate. The leader must keep an eye on individual performances even while holding the mission as the first priority. Although emotionally involved in the issues, the leader must stand back from the situation and make the choices that ensure that the missions are carried out and the best possible solutions to the problems are achieved. If, in an extreme situation, that means sacrificing the leader's or others' careers, health, or lives for the greater good of the largest number of people, or the greater good of the mission, a true leader must be willing to make that choice—or those choices. Such situations often occur in combat.

The parallel between combat leadership and crisis leadership is close, although lives are not always endangered in peacetime crises. Nevertheless, there are the same tensions, the same need for flexibility and innovation, and the same need to keep things basic and simple when tasking individuals and subordinate organizations to carry out responsibilities. The motivational leadership required in combat often is needed in a peacetime crisis to ensure that individuals work in close harmony. In combat, if soldiers think they have a real chance to succeed, if they trust and respect their leaders, if they have a feeling of individual invulnerability, if they believe the enemy will die, not them, they are more likely to be victorious. Leaders during crises need to operate in a well trained, yet pragmatic, way; they must not be tied inflexibly to the policies of the past that may not apply to fast-moving situations of the present.

A crisis often provides a very severe test of the horizontal and vertical cohesion of an organization. Organizations that are well led and well managed, that have worked hard to pull peer groups together (horizontal cohesion) and to ensure close and warm relationships between intermediate-level supervisors and their subordinates (vertical cohesion) often do well in a crisis. In fact, these organizations can be strengthened by a crisis because many learn from the experience and take pride that they have performed well during the stressful experience. For instance, the Tylenol poisoning crisis made Johnson & Johnson stronger since the company performed quickly and maturely. The public image of the company was enhanced as it developed better anti-tampering devices for its drugs and the leaders did not overreact to the criticism the company received.

One of the most useful techniques for a leader to employ in a crisis is to develop an "opportunity team" or teams, which are not directly involved in the moment-by-moment management of the crisis, but are close enough to the situation to be able to sit back, analyze opportunities, and suggest actions. Because leaders are so busy managing the crisis, they usually have no time to generate ideas on using the crisis to accomplish things that could not be done in non-crisis situations. A small group of innovators, perhaps the corporate long-range planning group, can provide the input of "why don't we try this?" or "have you thought of this option?" This technique can turn a crisis, which is both a challenge and a unique event, into an opportunity for the leader and for the organization.

An excellent example of a leader taking advantage of a crisis was President Kennedy during the Berlin Wall crisis of 1961. He used that crisis as an opportunity to build up conventional forces, to call reserves into active duty, and to deploy units to Europe on short notice for training and deterrent value. He had an "opportunity plan" and he carried it out. Franklin Roosevelt also took advantage of various world crises in the late 1930s and early 1940s to help prepare the United States for war. The initiation of a peacetime draft, lend-lease, and the "destroyer deal" are three examples.

After a crisis is over, it is useful to conduct a "hot washup" (a wonderfully descriptive term used throughout the NATO Alliance) which brings together the key people involved in the crisis to analyze what lessons were learned. In addition, an after-action report should be completed with an analysis of points or areas where future crises can be handled better.

A caution is in order here. Some leaders so thrive in a crisis environment that if one does not exist they will often create one themselves! This can be a useful technique for gaining the attention of lethargic employees and getting them to work at a high level of commitment and energy. On the other hand, creating crises can be quite disruptive and counterproductive. Creating crises can lead to cynicism and disgruntlement on the part of subordinates. They will roll their eyes up to the ceiling and say under their breaths, "Here we go again."

If as a leader you notice that you are just going from crisis to crisis you might ask yourself how many of these crises are generated from within the organization itself. Who knows—it may be your subordinates creating crises just to keep you busy or happy!

7

DEALING WITH THE DOWN SIDE

failures, rumors, criticism, and stepping down

Don't be discouraged by a failure. It can be a positive experience. Failure is, in a sense, the highway to success, inasmuch as every discovery of what is false leads us to seek earnestly after what is true, and every fresh experience points out some form of error which we shall afterwards carefully avoid.

—John Keats

A thick skin is a gift of God.

—Conrad Adenauer

Leaders of large organizations spend considerable time dealing with the unhappy side of human relationships. Problems will surface; it is the responsibility of leaders to ensure that they maintain good feedback loops relating to unfortunate events occurring within their organizations. These feedback loops should be even better than those dealing with more normal and upbeat events. Leaders must actively seek out bad news, but should understand that there will be people at various levels trying to withhold such news from them. The information they do receive often will be just a portion of the total bad news within their organizations.

All leaders of large organizations should fully understand that somewhere within their organizations there are often events occurring that have either unethical or illegal aspects. No matter how perceptive, aware, and "tuned in" leaders may be, they must realize that there are illegal, unethical, or unfortunate activities going on that go unreported. Sexual harassment, racial slurs, petty theft, drug abuse, alcoholism, and such, are the stuff of everyday life in many large organizations. Leaders must ensure that they have the procedures and the institutional support (auditors, health care professionals, lawyers, crisis action teams, etc.) available to identify these problems and solve them as expeditiously as possible.

There should be regular interaction with the lawyer or lawyers who work directly for the leader. Lawyers should be willing, able, and encouraged to be absolutely frank in their discussions with the leader. Decisions need to be made on a regular basis as to whether an accused party needs to be given appropriate administrative punishment, counselled, or fired. On occasion, decisions need to be made about family members and how they can be properly counselled. Advice from your lawyer is similarly helpful concerning activities that someone in the organization is trying to do for the greater good of the organization but which might be illegal or unethical in the given circumstances: for example, fund-raising activities such as Bingo games, raffles, slot machines, etc., that are prohibited by state or federal law; or, in overseas areas, by local law or status of forces agreements.

The lawyer should be a very important advisor, an individual who has a high level of integrity, is energetic and "tuned in," and believes in maintaining an appropriate balance between the rights of individuals and those individuals' obligations to the organization. Leaders should listen carefully to their lawyers and although, at times, a leader may want to overrule them, this should be done with great care. An individual with substantial legal training and experience can contribute greatly to the leader's thinking and decisionmaking.

Some leaders moan and groan whenever the subject of rumors, rumormongers, and the rumor mill comes up for discussion. Yet rumors can be very useful in large organizations and very helpful to leaders in a number of ways. If the leader stays tapped into the rumor mill, he or she will learn a lot. Many rumors are factual or at least are based on some factual data. Others give blazing insights as to where problems may be within the organization. Others are wrong—and some can be dangerous—but even these can be quite helpful, for they may alert the leader to an area that deserves immediate attention. The leader can often stamp out the rumor quickly with decisions or facts (or both) before it does too much damage.

As I mentioned in Chapter 6, at least one principal of a large high school plants ideas and information into the rumor mill with excellent results. For instance, suppose he gets the word that some of his students are planning to get together that afternoon, drive over to a rival school, and beat up some of the students for some perceived wrong of the past few days. Rather than announcing publicly his concerns and turning the issue into a confrontation between himself and some highly emotional students, he plants the word with some well informed students that he will expel permanently anyone who goes onto the other campus and does harm to person or property. The students then know that he is tuned in, that he has laid down a very specific threat, and that he has the power to carry it out. They may also suspect that he has notified the other school and that police may be waiting. The deterrence value of this approach can be quite powerful. The principal must of course be willing to follow up on his threat, and he must be sure that the school system superintendent and his school board will back him up.

One of the types of rumors that predominate many large organizations relates to personnel actions. X is about to be fired, Y is in line for that vacant vice president's job, Z will be the next big boss. Unfortunately, these rumors can sometimes cause individuals a lot of unnecessary trauma, concern, and disappointment. Yet it is impossible to stop them from spreading. A top executive can, however, reduce the number and the impact of personnel rumors by being decisive, realistic, and, most of all, honest. A leader who procrastinates on personnel actions, allows a cumbersome and lengthy personnel selection and promotion system to develop, or who insists upon clearing every personnel action, builds in time delays and encourages rumors. Leaders sometimes forget that through their indecisiveness or procrastination they are directly responsible for heartbreak when a rumor circulates about someone's promotion or great new job that does not materialize. One approach I have taken with my key staff members and subordinate leaders in this regard is as follows: "We all know that there are many important personnel activities coming up this summer. There is no way we can stop the rumors between now and the time that the big boss makes up his [or her] mind. If you don't know anything and want to speculate be my guest. However, if you are privy to inside information, please don't say anything to anybody. If the boss changes his [or her] mind some people may be terribly disappointed."

One more insight about rumors and promotion that comes from my personal experience. . . . In the Fall of 1978, I was commanding the 36th Tactical Fighter Wing in Europe. Almost all of the previous commanders had been selected for general officer while they held that marvelous command position. Rumors circulated widely that I would be promoted to brigadier general on the upcoming list. I had the job that I had dreamed of having for many years and had only been in command for a few months. I knew that if I was promoted that I would move on to a much less rewarding staff position. I strongly hoped that I would not be promoted that year, and that if promotion came, it would come after I had held command for at least a year and a half. Yet the promotion, which did come that same year, was not only a signal of my professional success but a signal to the wing that it was doing its job very well and had "gotten the boss promoted." Hence I let the rumors circulate and enjoyed the collective joy that the wing felt when the boss was on the "list." But it was with heavy heart and lots of withdrawal pains that I left the wing a few months later.

Leaders in top executive positions sometimes develop a siege mentality because they receive criticism from so many sources and with such frequency. This siege mentality on occasion causes executives to reject all criticism, even though some of it is very valid and very useful. An example from my own personal experience may help demonstrate the point about the frequency and unfairness of criticism. In the mid-1970s the United States Air Force developed a lightweight fighter, the YF–16. It won a competition with another experimental fighter and was selected by the United States Air Force and a number of NATO nations as the multipurpose fighter for the '70s, '80s, '90s, and beyond. To satisfy the needs of the European nations that were building portions of this aircraft in Europe, Deputy Secretary of Defense Bill Clements wanted to establish a specific price and configuration for this aircraft. But he didn't want to micromanage the program and he wanted to be scrupulously fair to the United States Air Force in establishing the guidelines. He asked me, as his Air Force military assistant, to work closely with the Air Force to make sure that his written guidance was fully acceptable. I came up with the idea that the Air Force write the guidance and Clements agreed. The Air Force senior leadership wrote a one-paragraph document, and Clements signed it without changing a word. Within a few weeks he was receiving very heavy criticism from many sources within the Air Force for the guidance he had issued. I found this to be quite unfair and told some very senior and some not-so-senior officers in the Air Force that the Deputy Secretary of Defense was getting a bum rap. Nevertheless the criticism continued. Needless to say, this heavy criticism did not help the Air Force in its relationship with the Deputy Secretary of Defense from that point onward. Clements later told me that he did not like and did not trust the top leaders in the Air Force, and nothing that I could say or do would change that situation. Unfair media criticism hurts, but unfair criticism from within the organization hurts even more. A top leader must indeed have a tough skin while, at the same time, remaining sensitive and responsive to fair and useful criticism.

It is the mature leader, indeed, who accepts even unfair criticisms with equanimity, calmness, and grace.

Those individuals who have reached high leadership positions without one or more major setbacks in their careers are often not well equipped to handle failure and heavy criticism. Therefore, when you are choosing individuals for leadership jobs, you may wish to look into their backgrounds to see if they have met failure and if so, how well they handled it.

When an organization suffers a major setback, the leader should be quick to accept the blame. It is the leader's fault that the organization failed because of poor planning, poor leadership, poor organization, or the inability to anticipate potential problems. There is always a temptation to blame subordinates, fate, poor quality of the equipment, lack of guidance from above, or overtasking. The leader should avoid these temptations. To quote the great Alabama football coach, the late Bear Bryant, "There's just three things I ever say. If anything goes bad, then I did it. If anything goes semi-good, then we did it. If anything goes really good, then you did it. That's all it takes to get people to win football games."

Fear of failure is one of the major causes of executive stress. A leader of a large organization should welcome an occasional failure. Failure often demonstrates that the organization is trying new approaches, setting ambitious goals, being innovative and creative, and avoiding "stand-patism" and "status-quoism." If leaders of large organizations take their subordinates on an annual off-site retreat, the failures of the past year should be discussed in a very positive way. The leader should compliment the group on the many new approaches taken, identify some of the failures as "heroic failures which taught us all" and those which, at a later time, may turn into grand successes. The leader ought to help everyone bounce back from failure. By doing so, he or she can encourage subordinates to continue to reach beyond their grasp in order to accomplish great things.

Soviet military philosophy on leadership raises the important point that the higher the post you occupy, the more strictly you will be judged. A leader is bound to be criticized, both fairly and unfairly, by subordinates within the organization, by his or her bosses and their staffs, by competitive organizations, and by the press. A leader who becomes very thin-skinned when criticized, or who becomes defensive and somewhat paranoid, is doing a disservice to the organization. By admitting failure early on, the leaders of an organization can often put it behind them, take necessary corrective action, and return the organization to a higher level of performance and morale. As a leader, it is important to observe your subordinate leaders and ascertain how well they accept criticism and how willing they are to accept blame for the failures of the organization. The defensive, thin-skinned, "blame-someone-else" individual is unlikely to succeed as a leader of a large organization.

Anyone who has ever trained for and run a complete marathon knows what it is like to hit the "wall" somewhere around the 20-mile mark in the 26-plus-mile race. Every muscle in the body cramps up and it is a real test of will to continue because the pain and agony is so severe. Leaders who step down from top leadership positions often experience similar problems, although the agony is mental and emotional rather than physical. Commonly called "withdrawal pains," the stepping down from an immensely rewarding executive position can be one of the most severe emotional experiences of a person's lifetime. Since it can be so bad, it deserves a few paragraphs in this book on leadership.

It is important for all leaders to understand the psychological impact that giving up a leadership job has. For all the frustrations, long hours, after-midnight phone calls, and multiple crises, leading is, in most cases, a very uplifting and rewarding experience. Therefore the stepping down from a leadership position, particularly one with lots of perks (executive secretaries, chauffeured cars, distinguished visitor treatment on trips, etc.) can be very traumatic indeed. Many leaders step down from one leadership job to go immediately to another, but some leave to return to marketing, teaching, staff duties, etc. Others will retire. This is where the trauma can be severe.

It is useful to think through these withdrawal problems in order to help you deal with the many pitfalls that may await you. One common tendency is to look back on the past leadership experience through rose-colored glasses and assume that your "reign" was one of extraordinary accomplishment, high employee morale, and exceptional style and grace. The result is often a feeling that the individual who replaced you is doing a lousy job and is screwing up the marvelous institution that you created.

Since your next job may not have a very full in-box or a very heavy speaking schedule, and may lack some of the psychic rewards that your previous leadership job had, you may find yourself in a state of depression and your performance in the new job may suffer. Since your company may have great plans for you in the future and you may have high ambitions yourself, it is important to overcome these periods of depression.

This is one of the many reasons that leaders should develop rewarding hobbies that can carry them through psychologically during the quiet times of their professional careers. The executives who give their entire mind, body, and soul to their work may succeed in the short run but may fail in the longer term. One must realize that one of the down sides of leadership is the trauma of withdrawal, and be prepared for it.

8

COMPLIMENTING CREATIVELY

saying thank you in many ways

When you first arrive at work, compliment someone; at lunch time find another to compliment; before you go home at night be sure to pay a compliment to someone else.

—Fred Kyler

A compliment is something like a kiss through a veil.

—Victor Hugo

Good leaders spend considerable time complimenting and thanking the people who work for them. It is quite an art to do this in a way that conveys sincerity, compliments people who should be complimented, and subtly leaves out people who do not deserve to be thanked or commended.

Casey Kasem, the radio disc jockey, introduces the Top 40 songs to his listening audience with great enthusiasm. One of the reasons for Kasem's success and popularity is his ability to find *uniqueness* in each song that makes the Top 40. A combination of his creativity, his commitment to research, and his love for his work make many people want to listen to his show.

A few years ago, he made the point that this was the first time in the history of the Top 40 that a Scottish trio, singing a country-western song, had made it to the Top 10. This introduction triggered a leadership idea. The following week, I made the point to all my subordinate leaders that they should look around at positive things their units had been doing that were unusual or special. By careful research and brainstorming, they were able to find, within our squadron and units, things that were unique or were establishing new standards or setting new records. We were able to highlight these things in the weekly base newspaper with headlines and laudatory stories: "Supply Squadron Establishes Record for Servicing F-15's"; "Security Police Set New Record in Processing of Licenses for Automobiles"; "Fighter Squadron and Maintenance Unit Set New Flying Time (or Sortie) Record," etc. This is a marvelous way to make people feel very special every week; it is a creative way to pay compliments. Many leaders just say "you all did well," "I'm proud of you," or "thanks a lot" in redundant ways. Making the "compliment-paying" aspect of your leadership more personal and creative pays dividends in individual and organizational morale. The idea of catching people doing things right rather than catching them doing something wrong has universal application.

Leaders should be sensitive to the great advantage of immediate recognition. They should have compliments, awards, bonuses, and medals at the ready, so when someone does something extraordinary (or something ordinary in an extraordinary way or with extraordinary results) immediate recognition can result.

In most organizations, 80 to 90 percent of the people are working very hard to accomplish the mission, to serve the institution, to make the unit look good, or to make you look good. People generally want to associate with, and participate in, success. It is important to remind yourself that your people are out there working hard and doing a fine job. You should spend a lot of time with these people, complimenting and thanking them. Occasionally when you get people together and praise them, there may be some who do not deserve your praise, but that fact should not deter you from complimenting the group. Individuals not deserving of praise can be dealt with separately and individually. When you thank your people, don't sound angry. Unfortunately, leaders on occasion get up and try to thank their people and it sounds like they are chewing them out. These leaders have not developed the kind of presence that permits them to reach out and figuratively wrap their arms around people to let them know that they respect and appreciate what they are doing. The brilliant, efficient individuals who cannot warmly thank, compliment, and commend their people will always fall well short of their full potential as leaders.

In the area of creative compliments, some thought should be given by a leader to developing techniques for complimenting subordinates individually as well as collectively. One of the highest compliments I've ever received was given to me by the late General Jerry O'Malley. He told me that the reason he had chosen me to be the Air Force Planner was because the majors and lieutenant colonels in the Plans Directorate had wanted me. By avoiding the normal rationale and finding a creative way to compliment me, he really touched me. It was as nice a compliment as I could have imagined. It came from a man who had a great understanding of people.

Of all the communications skills a leader should develop, praising creatively should be at the top of the list. Leaders should follow the advice of Letitia Baldridge: "Learn how to pay compliments. Start with members of your family, and you will find it will become easier later in life to compliment others. It's a great asset."

Short handwritten notes that the executive writes are usually greatly appreciated. "I have been thinking about your suggestion at the last staff meeting and I think it is superb. I plan to take action on it soon. Many thanks." or "Congratulations on your birthday. Your contributions over the past year have been first rate. I hope you enjoy working here as much as we enjoy having you part of our corporate family. It is a great privilege for me to share ideas with and learn from you."

Compliments can be a very powerful tool in motivating people to perform at higher levels of excellence and cooperation. This is especially true of the compliments that are well timed and well phrased. Conversely, the absence of compliments can be devastating to an organization. Too many leaders take the attitude that their people are "only doing their job" or "but that's what they get paid for." The hidden price that these leaders pay is low morale and a reduced level of performance.

Since many followers also value praise from their peers and from their subordinates, a leader should look for ways to feed his compliments back through the organization. One useful technique that I have used many times is whenever a subordinate tells me about how another subordinate has done a fine job, I say, "Thanks for telling me; I'll thank him [or her] personally—but I would ask you to pass on that praise to him [or her] yourself also."

A leader must also know how to accept compliments. An excellent guide is to pass every compliment you receive on to your subordinates for, in almost all cases, the success was theirs—their ideas, their efficiency, their hard work, and their creativity—all in marvelous combinations.

An important part of thanking and commending people is knowing their names. In very large organizations it is impossible for leaders to know most of their subordinates' names, but whenever they are about to present awards, compliment an organization publicly, or give a speech to a significant number of subordinates, they should mention a few names of people in the group who are particularly deserving of praise. Leaders must do their homework well in this regard and, if possible, meet briefly ahead of time with those individuals they are going to single out publicly. Leaders should ask lots of questions ahead of time, such as:

- Has the organization received any outside recognition lately?
- Has anyone in the audience done anything particularly noteworthy lately?
    - saved someone's life
    - recovered from major surgery
    - gotten married
    - had a baby
    - returned to work after a long absence
    - been elected to some important position

- Has the organization recently won a major sports event?
    - softball tournament

—golf match
—tennis tournament

If you can, take these individuals out to lunch, hold a seminar with them to get their ideas, or, in general, spend some time with them. During your time with them, call them by their first names. Benefits will rebound throughout the organization.

A leader can "pair" or "bond" with individuals at lower levels in his or her organization by using these techniques. As these individuals return to their workplaces they will spread the word that you were approachable, knew their names, showed interest in their ideas. This bonding will lead to greater trust and loyalty throughout the organization. If you know your people's hopes and dreams, if you understand and empathize with their hardships and complaints, you can better thank and compliment them and, just as importantly, you can better plan and make decisions for the good of the organization and the people that you serve.

9

DECENTRALIZING AND GETTING FEEDBACK
a twin dilemma

Strange as it sounds, great leaders gain authority by giving it away.

—James Stockdale

It does an organization no good when its leader refuses to share his leadership function with his lieutenants. The more centers of leadership you find in a company, the stronger it will become.

—David Ogilvey

There is a great deal of discussion in the literature on leadership that pertains to centralization versus decentralization. Most well-run organizations have a balanced amount of centralization and decentralization. At each level, there should be a certain amount of decisionmaking authority and a certain amount of delegation. The best leaders have a solid grasp of all the levels of decisionmaking and authority. They know which decisions should be made at each level and they let the various subordinate leaders know when they feel that decisions are being made at the appropriate level.

An essential element of the decentralization and delegating process is making sure that subordinates understand the organizational values, the goals and priorities, and the "big picture." This is an ongoing process with the top executive playing an important role as a teacher and reinforcer of the values that he or she holds dear. Decentralization and delegation does not mean the top leader becomes invisible or disengaged; only that the hand on the tiller is a light one.

It is important for subordinates at all levels to get psychic rewards from the work they do, from the authority they have, and from the decisions they make. Subordinate leaders should feel responsible and important. With the general trend in America toward better communication and more centralization, all leaders must work deliberately to force decisions down to the appropriate levels.

A twin dilemma emerges as a direct result of the marvelous communications and diversity of feedback mechanisms in large modern organizations. The process often takes place as follows: A new leader takes over, reorganizes the company to enhance decentralization, articulates a philosophy of empowerment of subordinate leaders, and establishes some excellent feedback mechanisms in order to stay in touch with activities throughout the organization. As the feedback loops give the leader lots of information, he or she tends to jump into problem areas or areas of personal interest. Soon the leader is aggressively recentralizing the organization so he or she can make lots of decisions that subordinate leaders should be making.

How can the leader strike the proper balance between centralization and decentralization? One solution to this dilemma is for the leader to accept the feedback with equanimity and to use this information to stay in touch with employees' concerns and ideas; to help accomplish his or her planning; to ask questions of subordinate leaders; and, on rare occasions, to jump into an issue or problem personally. When the leader does decide to get directly involved, he or she should work closely with the surbordinate leaders who normally have responsibility for this area. In addition, the leader should extract himself or herself from the details of the issue as soon as possible. Subordinate leaders should be given back the authority and responsibility for taking care of details. The point is an important one. Leaders should stay in touch and stay involved; but, on the other hand, they must discipline themselves constantly or they will slide down the slippery slope of continuous micromanagement of many areas. Micromanagement, the compulsive inclination to get into an infinite number of unimportant details, is seldom productive for leaders.

Within the context of an organization that has the proper amount of decentralization, leaders must ensure that they have a number of effective feedback mechanisms so that they can be apprised of important events that are going on within their organizations. The normal hierarchical structure (or chain of command in the military) that provides feedback is fine, but other means are needed to supplement it.

An inspection system and an auditing system are methods by which the leader can attain essential information. The leader and the organization's chief inspector and auditor should have a close relationship. It is important for the chief inspector and auditor to tell only the whole and unvarnished truth. The inspection systems within the organization must be staffed with excellent people who, because of their recognized competence, have the respect of individuals at all levels. The inspection system must emphasize integrity and not deteriorate into a pattern of activity that encourages prevarications and the withholding of important information. Self-inspection systems within subordinate organizations also can be effective tools. The leader should show interest in and support for such systems and ask for periodic reports on problem areas uncovered by these self-inspection systems.

Management control systems, which allow a great deal of quantifiable data to reach the leader, are also useful feedback mechanisms. However, in their worst forms, they can become heavy burdens on subordinates, detract from the mission, and deteriorate into exercises in data manipulation and dishonest reporting. A leader who has a computer on the desk where all kinds of information within the organization can be called up should never feel secure that the information is timely or accurate. If the information in this computer system is found to be inaccurate or dishonest, the leader should shut down the system or take corrective action to be sure the information flow becomes an effective means to help lead and manage the organization. A leader should periodically have an outside agency examine the management control system in detail to be sure it is serving the desires of the leader and the mission of the organization.

Executives should periodically delve into reports that staff agencies are submitting to higher headquarters. These reports are often the source of pressures on subordinates to violate their integrity. In other words, it is not only reports to you, but also the reports to corporate headquarters, that can be a source of the breakdown of personal and institutional integrity.

Subordinates can identify the phony leaders in very rapid order and are therefore an excellent source for insight about subordinate leaders working for you. A subordinate leader who may look wonderful to you may look very different when viewed from below. Walt Ulmer, President of The Center for Creative Leadership, who has held many top executive positions, feels that there should be some subordinate input into personnel evaluations. Although this may be impracticable in a formal sense, there is a great deal of wisdom in Ulmer's point. Informal mechanisms can be helpful in ensuring that the top leader does not tolerate abysmal leadership on the part of one or more of his subordinate leaders.

Informal feedback through individuals who are not in the organizational hierarchy and who do not work directly for the top leader also can be effective. Retired individuals who are keeping in close touch with many of their friends who remain within the organization can be good sources of mature and objective feedback. The "spouses' net" can provide valuable insights. Additionally, there are almost always individuals who are so "tuned in" that they can be helpful even though they do not occupy key positions within the hierarchical structure.

A president of a multibillion dollar corporation shared with me that the way he stays in touch is through lots of off-the-record phone calls from friends throughout his company and throughout his industry. This man, who is a dear friend, is a person of such extraordinary kindness and thoughtfulness that it is easy to see why he has such a vast network of friends and information. People like him and enjoy staying in contact with him and keeping him informed.

Leaders should be careful how they use informal means of

feedback. They must support subordinate leaders and must not violate the established rules of hierarchy. On the other hand, not utilizing informal means of feedback can be a mistake. Without good feedback from many sources, the leader of a large organization is partially blind and, over time, can become isolated from the real problems and the real issues. Isolation diminishes a leader's ability to anticipate problems, to receive innovative ideas, to maximize opportunities, and to serve as an enlightened and creative leader.

A leader should be particularly sensitive to feedback from groups within the organization that may feel both collectively and individually that they are "second-class citizens." If not given proper attention, these groups can become a source of poor morale and poor performance. The dilemma here is that determined and consistent decentralization can lead to neglect of certain groups, including racial and ethnic minorities, and administrative, maintenance, and clerical personnel. The executive should take special care to give these people time, support, and loving care, even though, by doing so, he or she may be violating, to some degree, the desirable policy of decentralization.

Minorities can provide enormous strength to an organization by bringing a diversity of cultural experiences and a certain cohesiveness within each group. A wise executive can take advantage of these strengths if he or she pursues an enlightened policy toward equal opportunity and fair treatment. The leader should make himself or herself available to informal leaders of various minority groups to obtain feedback and ideas from these influential leaders.

When I had 400 blacks and about 100 Hispanics under my command at Bitburg, I attended many dinners and preached in gospel religious services (my wife sang solos in various church services). These activities permitted me to stay in touch with two very cohesive and very supportive groups.

Leaders should remind themselves periodically that minority groups and individuals are "eternally visible." As Admiral Paul Reason, a bright and articulate black officer, says, "If you do something right, everyone will notice; if you do something wrong, everyone will notice."

This very high visibility tends to put extra pressure on any person who can easily be recognized by skin color or gender. In one sense, all leaders share some of this pressure, since they are also highly visible. Hence leaders can "bond" with subordinates from minority groups because they have this "visibility factor" in common.

Leaders who are women or who come from racial or ethnic minority groups have an advantage in this general area, since it becomes relatively easy for them to get good feedback from other members of the organization who are of the same gender or minority group. But these leaders face a reverse dilemma; that is, how to ensure that the "white male" feedback loops operate effectively. These leaders need to stay in close contact with key subordinates who are, in turn, in close contact with these more traditional feedback loops.

The whole issue of equal opportunity for racial and ethnic minorities, women, and bachelors will become even more important in the future than it has been in the past. Too many of the top leaders in this country, who consider themselves to be quite enlightened, in fact carry deep within them some very heavy prejudices in one or more of these areas. As you look around your major meetings you should ask yourself periodically how many women, bachelors, and members of minority groups are present and in what numbers. In counselling sessions with your subordinates, you should raise the issue of minorities in key positions. An enlightened leader will construct a training and development program that will bring minorities along, so that in the long-term future of the organization the various subcultural elements within the organization will be properly represented in the highest positions. A program such as this is not only the right thing to do: it is also functionally sound, for no organizations can maximize the vital feedback mechanism if only males from a single race sit around the corporate and organizational boardrooms of the nations of the world.

10

MAKING THE BIG DECISIONS
five useful checks

In the long run men hit only what they aim at.
>—Henry David Thoreau

After all is said and done, there is a lot more said than done.
>—Anonymous

From my experience in government and from observing at rather close hand a number of large businesses, it is my judgment that most top executives try to make too many decisions. Most decisions in a large organization should be made at levels below the top, the leaders should reserve their precious time for the really key or sensitive decisions. It is the wise leader, indeed, who focuses most of his or her attention on the big decisions (a dozen or so each year) and decisions on particularly sensitive issues (perhaps another dozen). If leaders make a much greater number of decisions, generally they are either unable to get into the issues to fully understand what they are deciding, or unable to follow up properly to ensure that the implementation process carries out the letter and spirit of the decisions. In other words, if a leader tries to do too much he or she will, in the long run, accomplish too little.

Before a decision is made by a top executive, he or she should ensure that complete coordination has taken place and that all important players both inside and outside the organization have had an opportunity to express fully their views. At any decision meeting the leader should reemphasize the "no nonconcurrence through silence" rule in order to draw out the views of quiet skeptics who worry about the direction that the leader may be taking and can offer some useful cautionary comments about the thrust of his or her thinking.

The leader should, before making a final decision, accomplish five important checks: the Sanity Check, the Dignity Check, the Systems Check, the *Washington Post* Check, and the Integrity Check. This 5-check rule of thumb has served me well not only as a leader but also as a subordinate and adviser to senior executives.

☐**The Sanity Check** is very simple but quite important. Now that the agony of the coordination process is over and now that all the delicate compromises have been made to get the key agencies and individuals to support the tentative decision, does the decision make sense? Have we created a thoroughbred racehorse, a plodding but sturdy farm horse or a multi-humped camel? The leader may find that the best he or she can get is the farm horse and may well have to be satisfied with that. But he should not accept the camel. The best example I know of this problem is the coordination and decision process in the Office of the Joint Chiefs of Staff. This process produces a very high percentage of camels. When I was the Military Assistant to the Deputy Secretary of Defense I could not get the Deputy Secretary (Bill Clements—later to be Governor of Texas on two occasions) to read any of the major JCS documents. In his judgment, which I shared, they were so heavily compromised as to be almost worthless. If the decision doesn't make sense then it is the obligation of the leader to reject it and to give guidance to the staff on how to proceed. It is not fair to the staff to reject a carefully compromised and coordinated decision paper without providing some guidance on where to proceed.

☐**The Dignity Check** is also quite simple. Will this decision enhance the reputation and dignity of this organization and its leadership, or will it undermine that reputation? If the latter is the case—if the decision "smells bad"—the leader should return the issue for further staff consideration and provide subordinates with some "top-down" guidance on what he or she objects to and suggestions on how to fix the problems.

☐**The Systems Check** requires a careful consideration of the various parts of the decision to ensure that there is internal consistency and coherency and that this decision also fits within the overall goals and priorities of the organization. Even though individual parts of the decision may make sense when analyzed separately, all the parts must fit together if the decision is to have any chance of being implemented in a way that will serve the interests of the leader and the organization. Part of the Systems Check is to check the tentative decision with the strategic plan to make sure this decision is in furtherance of the mission of the organization. If I may use an airplane analogy: the wings, fuselage, engines, cockpit, landing gear, and pilot must all fit nicely together or the airplane (or decision) will not fly—or, if it does fly, it will not fly smoothly.

☐**The Washington Post Check** (or the Jack Anderson, or, perhaps, the *Miami Herald* Check) is also quite straightforward. How will this decision appear when it is written up by a media critic? From my many years of work in the Pentagon, I have found this argument the most useful one in stopping superiors from making dumb decisions. One useful technique is to try to frame a very critical headline and at the appropriate time to raise the issue this way: "I can see the headline in the paper next week—'Department of Defense Decides to Change the Name of the National War College: Curriculum Stays the Same—Still Studying War; Another Example of Defense Department Deception?'" The media gets so much criticism and much of it is deserved, but if it wasn't for the media the number of stupid decisions made in government and elsewhere would increase significantly.

☐**The Integrity Check** is the basic ethics issue about both ends and means and about the long-term reputation of the organization. In the interest of pursuing legitimate goals, have we selected unethical means to beat the competition, to fool the press, to outsmart the Congress, or to beat the Japanese? Are the goals themselves ethical? The integrity check can be very useful as a deterrent to unethical behavior. If your subordinates know that you are going to do an ethical examination of the issue, they are much more likely to find ethical means to reach ethical ends.

All true leaders are agents of change as they create a strategic vision and take their organizations to higher levels of performance and excellence. The decisionmaking process is an important means by which leaders accomplish these goals. It is very useful for the leader to conceptualize about his or her approach to decisionmaking and to make it a systematic process. President Eisenhower had a great sense for where decisions ought to be made. Many decision papers were sent to him and he would reserve the important ones for himself. Many others he would send back to a Cabinet member and Agency head with a note saying, "I want you to decide this, I will support your decision." By disciplining his in-box and by husbanding his time for the really important and particularly sensitive issues, Ike established a model that other top executives in and out of government could do well to emulate.

Leaders who discipline themselves to the point that they are only making a few decisions each month have the time to check periodically on the coherency and consistency of their decisions, as well as to reflect upon the important interrelationship between their strategic vision and their decisions. Leaders who race around putting out fires may get lots of psychic rewards out of being extremely busy, but the price they pay—in reduced coherency and leadership vision—may be quite high. A leader should draw satisfaction not from the *quantity* of his or her decisions, but from their *quality*; satisfaction not out of just the decision itself, but out of its full implementation.

11

REACHING OUTWARD AND UPWARD
building bridges

A man should live with his superiors as he does with his fire; not too near, lest he burn, nor too far off, lest he freeze.

—Diogenes

We must all hang together, or assuredly we shall all hang separately.

—Benjamin Franklin

It is important for the leaders of large organizations not only to know their people and their missions well, to plan carefully, and to manage the solution of problems within the organization, but also to reach out to other organizations, to higher headquarters, to sister units, to the outside community, and to institutions that have important interactions with the organization. A leader should spend a considerable amount of time building bridges.

A useful formula to be followed is to treat sister organizations with warmth, respect, and affection. A leader is not serving the organization well if he or she permits or encourages "turf battles" with neighboring institutions. If the top leader figuratively embraces the leaders of major bureaucratic rivals and lets everyone in the organization know that nonconstructive criticism, backbiting, and turf battles will not be tolerated, many of the problems that exist between organizations will quickly disappear—whether the "rivalry" is between a mayor and the city council, between two production facilities in a manufacturing company, between branch offices of an international bank, between the planners and the programmers in the Pentagon, between the Army and the Air Force, or between the Department of Defense and the Department of State. When leaders pledge themselves to work cooperatively, they reduce considerably the risk of highly competitive individuals turning good, honest competition into dysfunctional criticism, parochialism, and unproductive opposition.

In working with higher headquarters, the leader must be loyal to those above him, knowledgeable concerning the key agencies and department heads, and cooperative with the staff members. The leader must keep an eye on those staff members and departments or agencies at the corporate or department headquarters who ask unreasonable things of people, put unwarranted pressures on the organization, and operate as if they were the ultimate leader. It is important for leaders of organizations at lower levels to stand up for their people, to contact the people or groups of people who are placing undue requirements on them, and to set standards for interaction that are appropriate within the organizational hierarchy or chain of command. Doing this delicately, and with mutual respect, is a difficult job, but one which leaders must address. It has been my experience that senior executives want to know how well their staff and subordinate organizations are working together. When leaders call attention to problem areas in a diplomatic way, and make appropriate suggestions for improvement through the chain of command, higher headquarters will be responsive and, in fact, appreciative of the input.

At the higher levels of very large organizations, outreach becomes almost an art form. The chemistry that develops between you, as a leader, and your boss greatly affects the relationship between the staff of the boss, your staff, and your subordinate organizations. If you can maintain an atmosphere of mutual trust and respect between you and your boss, as well as with top staff people, your subordinates will benefit. If, however, the chemistry between you and your boss is bad—or if his or her staff is constantly ''poisoning your well,'' you and your subordinates are in for a rough time. If your organization performs most of its duties, tasks, and missions in an outstanding way, trust and good chemistry are fairly easy to establish and maintain in most cases. It is your role to work hard to maintain that good chemistry between your organization and the next higher echelon.

It is important for the executive to help his or her subordinates understand that their job is not to fight with higher headquarters but to cooperate with the various staff agencies at a higher level. If there is a fight to be waged, leaders should gather the facts and engage in the battle themselves. In addition, they should not forget to let subordinates know how higher headquarters responds to the unit's performance, suggestions, and ideas.

Of course, leaders must be careful not to consider outreach their major objective. There are some leaders who spend so much time satisfying the boss above them, doing so much outreach to other organizations, and spending disproportionate amounts of time on diplomatic functions, that they spend too little time with the organizations they lead. These individuals become absentee leaders and, as a result, begin to lose the loyalty and support of the people who work for them. It is the mature leader who keeps outreach and "inreach" in proper balance. As in so many areas of leadership, what you do or how you do it is important, but so is a proper sense of proportion and balance.

12

PERSONALITY AND HEALTH TESTING
tools for enlightened leaders

The first trait that is common among those who are assured a place in history is that of being predisposed to continual self-improvement. Those who have it are dynamically regenerative.

—James Stockdale

*O wad some Power the giftie gie us
To see ourselves as others see us!*

—Robert Burns

Many executives feel that personality assessment tools are a great waste of time and money. From my extensive experience as a leader of both American and international organizations I have learned that personality assessment tools and health testing, used in combination with good judgment and a bit of honest skepticism, can be helpful to the executive in a number of important ways.

First, personality assessment tools can help the leader better understand that other styles and other ways of dealing with situations are not wrong—they are just different from what the leader might have done. Too many leaders think that different perspectives are erroneous perspectives and as a result they fail to fully capitalize on the strengths of subordinates who seem a little "different" or "strange."

Second, these tools can help leaders understand that they need to have diverse personalities on their executive teams to compensate for their own weaknesses and biases and to stretch their minds and open them to new possibilities and opportunities.

Third, by understanding people, the leader often can assign them to positions where their personality traits will be most productive. By understanding some of the better personality assessment tools, an executive has a framework to better understand the most important element of any organization, the people.

Fourth, personality assessment tools can be quite useful in the self-analysis and introspection process that all leaders should undertake periodically. See Chapter 13 and Appendix A, Checklist 13.

An important part of many of the executive development courses offered around the country is an assessment activity that administers a series of sophisticated tests designed to evaluate the various skills, personality preferences, and leadership styles of the participants. The assessments offer the participants a unique set of insights into their various strengths and weaknesses. The courses then afford them the opportunity to learn new skills that help to promote their strengths and assist in correcting their weaknesses.

One of the most popular assessment instruments, and my personal favorite, is the *Myers Briggs Type Indicator* (MBTI). The MBTI, which is published by the Consulting Psychologists Press, is based upon the typology of Carl Jung. The instrument measures personality styles and preferences along four continuums which further separate into sixteen categories. The categories further differentiate themselves based on the strengths of an individual's scores. The first continuum evaluates the individual in terms of extroversion or introversion. Jung, who coined these two terms, felt that this continuum represented the most powerful differences between people. The extrovert (E) thinks out loud in the world of people and things, while the introvert (I) processes information internally in the world of concepts and ideas. The second continuum in the MBTI deals with the ways that individuals gather information for the decisionmaking process. The first preference on this continuum is called sensing (S), because these individuals gather data with the five basic senses. The second preference is referred to as intuition (N), because these individuals prefer to leap over the tangibles and look for hidden meanings, relationships, and possibilities. The third continuum deals with opposite ways of deciding. The first preference is called thinking (T). These individuals make decisions fairly impersonally based upon an evaluation of cause and effect. The other end of this third continuum is called feeling (F); individuals with this style tend to make decisions based on personal values. The fourth and final continuum is the only dimension that is not directly drawn from Jungian theory, although it certainly complements it. This continuum, developed by the two authors of the MBTI, deals with differences between people in the use of perception and the use of judgment in dealing with the outer world. Individuals with judging (J) preference rely on a judging process, and tend to live in a planned, decided, orderly manner. They seek constantly to regulate and control their lives. The perceptive (P) individuals rely mainly on a perceptive process for dealing with the outer world, and live in a flexible and spontaneous manner. Their quest in life is understanding the meaning of life, and adapting to it. These four continuums in combination with one another make up the sixteen MBTI types.

The following table, taken from the book *Please Understand Me: An Essay on Temperament Styles* by David Keirsey and Marilyn Bates, illustrates the differences that are measured by the MBTI.

I am an "ENTJ" and have learned over the years the strengths and weaknesses of someone like me who is a strong Extrovert (E) and also a strongly Intuitive (N) person, as well as being a Thinker (T) and a Judger (J). My biggest two weaknesses as a leader are first my extroversion—I tend to be a poor listener since I love to talk a lot. My second big weakness relates to the fact that I am a T rather than an F. I come across to some as cold and uncaring—poor qualities for a leader.

Another useful test, the creation of Dr. Elias H. Porter, is the *Strength Deployment Inventory.* Though not yet well known, Porter's work is growing in popularity. Porter's test provides

MBTI: Personality Styles and Preferences

E (75% of the population)	*versus*	I (25% of the population)
Sociability		Territoriality
Interaction		Concentration
External		Internal
Breadth		Depth
Extensive		Intensive
Multiplicity of relationships		Limited relationships
Expenditure of energies		Conservation of energies
Interest in external events		Interest in internal reaction

S (75% of the population)	*versus*	N (25% of the population)
Experience		Hunches
Past		Future
Realistic		Speculative
Perspiration		Inspiration
Actual		Possible
Down-to-earth		Head-in-clouds
Utility		Fantasy
Fact		Fiction
Practicality		Ingenuity
Sensible		Imaginative

T (50% of the population)	*versus*	F (50% of the population)
Objective		Subjective
Principles		Values
Policy		Social values
Laws		Extenuating circumstances
Criterion		Intimacy
Firmness		Persuasion
Impersonal		Personal
Justice		Humane
Categories		Harmony
Standards		Good or bad
Critique		Appreciate
Analysis		Sympathy
Allocation		Devotion

J (50% of the population)	*versus*	P (50% of the population)
Settled		Pending
Decided		Gather more data
Fixed		Flexible
Plan ahead		Adapt as you go
Run one's life		Let life happen
Closure		Open options
Decision-making		Treasure hunting
Planned		Open ended
Completed		Emergent
Decisive		Tentative
Wrap it up		Something will turn up
Urgency		There's plenty of time
Deadline!		What deadline?
Get show on the road		Let's wait and see

From David Keirsey and Marilyn Bates, *Please Understand Me: An Essay on Temperament Styles* (Del Mar, CA: Prometheus Nemesis Books, 1978). Copyright © 1978, David Keirsey and Marilyn Bates. Reprinted by permission.

additional understanding and insights into one's individual behavior and the behavior of others. The instrument measures behavior, first under normal stress-free conditions, and, second, when the individual perceives conflict and opposition. These two scores are then displayed in a manner wherein the individuals can see their scores on a multidimensional continuum. While there are various possible combinations, the SDI indicates interpersonal styles clustered around the following orientations.

Altruistic-Nurturing

The basic value system of altruistic-nurturing individuals is a genuine concern for the protection, growth, and personal welfare of others. They strive to be open and responsive to the needs of others. This style is color coded *blue*.

Analytic-Autonomizing

Analytic-autonomizing individuals value the importance of a rational, analytical process and order. Their style is to be objective, in control of their emotions, cautious and thorough, fair and principled; they think things through before acting. They are color coded *green* on the instrument.

Assertive-Directing

The primary value system of assertive-directing individuals is a concern for task accomplishment and the organization of people and associated resources toward that end. Their style is toward leadership and persuasion, alert for opportunities, quick to claim the right to earned rewards, inclined to push for immediate action. They will challenge others, and will relish risk-taking. They are color coded *red* on the SDI.

Flexible-Cohering

The flexible-cohering individuals display a blend of the other three styles. They are not identified by a color and are referred to as *hubs* (or rainbows) since they are a true combination of all three. They are oriented to the importance of membership in groups and effective group behavior. They are curious about what others think and feel, are open-minded, and are willing to adapt and change. These individuals like to experiment with how to act, like to be members of groups, and like to be known as flexible.

Although some may feel that a Blue cannot be a strong leader, that is not the case at all. For instance, the United States Marine Corps, a service well respected for its fine leadership, has a very large number of Blues in its midst. Recently I uncovered someone who may be the ideal as far as a Blue leader. Martha Scroggs runs a parochial elementary school in Augusta, Georgia; in addition, she teaches the first grade. Each day between 7:40 and 8:15 she meets and greets by name over 400 enthusiastic children as they pile out of the cars and buses. She is not only the unofficial greeter—she is also the official tooth puller, having pulled more than 1,000 baby teeth over the years. Children with parents in hand willingly come to see her at night and on weekends when the tooth or teeth are "ready for Mrs. Scroggs." She does all this for the sheer joy of being with small children and her blueness helps make her a particularly effective leader.

Most people who take the Strength Deployment Inventory do not score in one of the four pure orientations described above. They find themselves to be combinations and mixes in a less pure form.

The Strength Deployment Inventory is useful because it categorizes individual orientations into groupings that are easy to understand. The most interesting insight that comes out of the SDI, in my judgment, is what happens to individuals when they are confronted or criticized. Behavior orientation often changes. For instance, I am basically Red-Blue: this means that I am a hard-driving, goal-setting, ambitious person, but that I also have some altruistic, caring qualities. My goal-setting qualities are more prominent than the altruistic qualities. When confronted, however, I adopt the analytical orientation (Green). I generally don't become angered—I get interested if someone criticizes me. It allows me to handle criticism somewhat less emotionally than people who turn Red when they are confronted and become angry. Those who turn Blue during conflict work hard to accommodate the criticism, to compromise, and to find ways to end the confrontation as soon as possible. If they cannot find accommodation, they will try to withdraw.

One of the newest evaluation devices is the "hot reactor" test which measures the relationship between psychological stress and physiological reactivity. The procedure looks at the relationship between stress and blood pressure. About 25 percent of American executives, when placed under mild psychological stress, have very high blood pressure readings. The procedure was developed by Dr. Robert Eliot, who is the Director of Preventative and Rehabilitative Cardiology at the Heart-Lung Center, St.Luke's Hospital in Phoenix, Arizona. The "hot reactor" test takes about forty-five minutes to administer. The subject is connected to an automatic blood pressure machine, then asked to engage in a series of mental activities. The performance on the assigned tasks is recorded as well as the blood pressures. During these activities, a significant number of individuals exhibit blood pressure levels that are significantly higher than their resting blood pressures. The procedure gives the subject an indication of what his or her actual blood pressure is during normal day-to-day activities. Leaders who fully understand the implications of the "hot reactor" test can do a great service to those subordinates who are doing major physical damage to themselves as a result of their reactions to ringing telephones, angry bosses, short deadlines, etc. These individuals can be helped with medical interventions and changes in work patterns and lifestyles. Leaders who are interested in the health of their organizations and the wellness of the people who work for them may wish to learn about the "hot reactor" test, and, if possible, make it available for subordinates.

It is clear from available and proven tests that physical and mental health are closely related. Health testing, like the personality assessment tools, can provide leaders with valuable information. People who are in regular exercise programs and who maintain good control of their work habits, diet, and weight, often have more to contribute in the long term to the goals of their institutions than those who are very overweight, or do not pay attention to their diet and health habits and, therefore, often work below potential performance levels. Treadmill stress tests, in coordination with a blood chemistry analysis, can determine quite precisely the "health age" of an individual. A fifty-year-old person who has a health-age of sixty-five may not contribute to an organization for many more years unless corrective action with regard to diet, exercise, excessive smoking and/or drinking, is taken soon. Leaders themselves should take these tests since the health of the leader has a great deal to do with the health of the organization. Also, by taking the tests, a leader shows interest in, and support for, the fitness program.

There is a close relationship between physical and mental health and between physical and mental vigor. For instance, many do their best thinking while walking or jogging, returning from their exercise with new vigor to attack the issues of the day, as well as with new ideas. If leaders are visible to subordinates as they pursue their exercise programs, they are likely to encourage others to get regular exercise.

As I welcome, every couple of weeks, each new group of people that comes to work for me, I say, "If I see you walking down the hall with an athletic bag in your hand that is good, not bad; take a few hours off each week for some vigorous exercise—you will be more productive in the long run." Look carefully at the exercise facilities available to the men and women who work for your organization: locker rooms and shower facilities, exercise rooms and intramural sports programs. Attention to this area can reap great benefits in performance and morale, as well as in mental and physical fitness.

In developing an organizational climate that emphasizes good mental and physical health, leaders should be mindful of the needs of the handicapped. As leaders plan to set up exercise rooms, sports programs, aerobics classes, treadmill testing, etc., they should also plan for comparable programs for the blind, the deaf, those confined to wheelchairs, and others who might feel left out of a standard company wellness program.

In addition to understanding individual psychological and physical factors, a wise leader will periodically examine the psychological climate of the organization. For instance, the National War College had an educational climate and a curriculum that heavily emphasized extroversion and intuition. Active learning (emphasized in the seminar environment), case study approaches, and political-military simulations, all favored the extrovert. The curriculum's emphasis on conceptualization, frameworks of analysis, and models favored the intuitive personality over the sensing personality. Since about half of our students are neither extroverts nor intuitives, they have been somewhat disadvantaged by this educational approach. By recognizing our bias in favor of individuals whose personality preferences include extroversion and intuition, the faculty has taken an important first step. The next step is more difficult: redesigning the academic program to accommodate the needs and desires of the introverts and sensors while preserving the excellence of the present program.

13

LOOKING AT YOURSELF
the importance of introspection

I worry about the self-made man who worships his maker.
                                    —*Bishop Stewart*

Half the CEOs of the world are below average.
                                    —*David Campbell*

Leaders should think of themselves as individuals surrounded by mirrors of many kinds. Many of these mirrors are distorted; some of them reflect back so leaders can judge themselves accurately, but many of them do not. Even the most consistent of leaders is many things to many people. Leaders should try to correct the worst of these distortions when possible. However, they must avoid becoming paranoid or defensive about the distortions they cannot correct. Herein lies the need for self-confidence and self-esteem combined with the willingness to listen, to accept criticism, to learn from mistakes. Leaders must realize that they are five people: who they are, who they think they are, and who they are perceived to be by their subordinates, peers, and superiors. In many cases, there is a close relationship between and among the five "yous." In other cases, the relationship is not close at all. Just as you are not as good-looking, sexy, brilliant, witty, or charismatic as you sometimes think you are, you may well be perceived in much less favorable light than the facts would support. If you very occasionally have one too many drinks, you will be perceived by many as a chronic alcoholic; if you occasionally close your eyes or nod off during a long, boring meeting, you will be perceived by many as suffering from incipient senility. if you occasionally fire a subordinate, you will be perceived as a leader who is constantly on the watch to find someone to fire. The true mature leader acknowledges these "perception gaps" and works hard to become introspective and to get feedback, and to take corrective action when appropriate.

Perhaps the greatest benefit that a leader gains from being objectively introspective is that it enhances executive performance. Leaders who know who they are, who recognize their strengths (and use these strengths to advantage), and who understand their weaknesses (and compensate for these weaknesses), perform much better than leaders who do not or cannot understand themselves. Introspective leaders can avoid some mistakes and can project the aura of self-confident leadership that elicits the respect of subordinates and support for the leader's initiatives.

Part of self-evaluation is listening to what you say and how you say it as well as understanding how your phrases and messages are received throughout the warp and woof of your organization. Leaders should avoid using phrases that send misleading or erroneous messages or diminish the dignity of the leader, his or her subordinates, and the organization itself. Commonly used phrases like "My door is always open" and "I don't like surprises," which may be fine for leaders of smaller organizations, may be very counterproductive for leaders of large organizations. Checklist 10 in Appendix A lists a number of phrases which top executives should generally avoid using because they send out misleading signals, reduce the dignity of the organization, establish an atmosphere of intimidation, or demonstrate a propensity towards micromanagement.

An executive needs to be introspective in order to avoid becoming, over time, out of touch, imperious, or somewhat irrelevant, and hence less effective as a leader. This introspection process should be accomplished systematically; it should be done regularly; and, it should be done with the help of someone else, whether it be the leader's executive secretary, deputy, executive assistant, trusted friend, or spouse.

Knowing who you are, what your ideals are, what your

psychological, spiritual, and religious strengths and weaknesses are, can help improve your ability to provide enlightened leadership. It is healthy and useful to periodically ask yourself: What values do I *really* think are worth committing myself to? What are my deeply held prejudices? Do I *really* practice what I preach?

Other important aspects of self-evaluation and introspection involve assessing your on-the-job effectiveness. These considerations are discussed in the balance of this chapter.

Establishing your schedule. How much time do you spend visiting on the shop floor, in the manufacturing and maintenance areas, or in the field? How much time do you spend with your subordinates watching or playing organized sports or participating in informal sports such as jogging? Do you attend social gatherings? Does your secretary keep a close track of your schedule and provide feedback as to how many hours each month you are spending in such aspects of your job? How many hours are you spending visiting subordinate and subsidiary units or attending meetings? What kind of meetings are they and who else attends those meetings? In my view, the four-hour rule, which recommends that leaders of large organizations should spend no more than four hours a day in the office, has great merit. The rest of the time should be spent meeting with other people, visiting subsidiary organizations, participating in or watching sports activities with subordinates, attending social events, conducting ceremonies, or giving short, substantive, motivational speeches.

Henry Brandon of the London *Times* made a critical point that has relevance for leaders of large organizations: "Americans tend to be influenced in their judgment of politicians and corporate executives by how much time they spend behind their desks. They do not attach enough importance to the advantages of the clarity of a relaxed mind."

Establishing your priorities. Do you and your people know what your priorities are? Have you written them down and discussed them with your subordinates? Do you follow your own priorities? Individuals in top leadership positions need to establish priorities for themselves and for their organizations. There should be a close correlation between the priorities of the individual in a leadership position and the priorities of the organization. After these priorities are articulated both in oral and written form, they should be followed by the leader. If you establish priorities that you are unwilling to follow, those priorities become a source of cynical comment.

Examining your reliability. How often do you cancel out at the last minute on a meeting, speech, ceremony, visit, sporting event, or social engagement? Once you make a commitment to do something, you should do it. Only an emergency, ill health, or some other serious crisis should cause you to cancel a commitment. Of course, in agreeing to do things, you should be careful not to over-schedule yourself, not to accept responsibilities that you can't fulfill, and not to doublebook a specific period. In Europe, I was impressed by the great respect the senior leaders from many nations had for the then Supreme Allied Commander in Europe, General Alexander M. Haig, Jr. When they were asked individually why they had such high regard for General Haig, the answer was always along the following lines, "Al Haig is reliable. If he says he is going to put a United States brigade in northern Germany, he puts a brigade in there. If he says he's going to make a speech for me, he makes a speech for me. If he says he's going to visit a certain unit, he visits that unit. Whether he's tired, whether he's sick, or whether he has other things on his mind, he lives up to his commitments. Al Haig is reliable and I respect him."

Who tells you all the news—good and bad? It is important for leaders to have around them people who are honest and forthright, who give them the bad news as well as the good news, and who do not play the role of sycophants when dealing with them. You need to sit down periodically and ask yourself: Who around me is willing to tell the full story? Is it your deputy, your executive assistant, your secretary, a trusted friend, your spouse, or your children? If there is no one, or if those voices are very weak, you should hire someone and put him or her very close to you so that you have someone to tell you when the "emperor has no clothes."

How long are your meetings? If you love to hear your own voice, your meetings can go on for hours and can waste an enormous amount of time for you and your key subordinates. Meetings should be short, brisk, and to the point, with a reasonable agenda set ahead of time and followed. A good basic rule on routine meetings is that they should not last more than one hour and, if there is to be a briefing, there should be no more than twenty slides used. If there is more than an hour's worth of business to be done, the meeting should be broken into parts. Long meetings are dysfunctional, tying up people and straining the attention span of many. You need to look at yourself and find out whether you have become, as many leaders do, enamored with your own words. Do you preach rather than listen?

How well do you listen? Listening is an acquired art. It requires self-discipline and well developed skills. Leaders should listen and listen and listen. Only through listening can they find out what's really going on. If someone comes in to raise an issue with the leader and the leader does not allow the individual to state the full case and to get emotions out in the open, the leader is likely to understand only a piece of the story and the problem probably will not be solved. In addition, the individual who brought in the problem will be frustrated because there was no opportunity to lay the whole issue on the table and to make sure the leader fully understood the problem. Passive listening, where the leader listens quietly and does not interrupt with comments or questions, is most appropriate when the individual wants to get something off his or her chest and doesn't want to be interrupted; passive listening is very important at times. Active listening—where the leader interrupts with questions occasionally—also can be a very useful way to keep track of what is being said, to make sure the case is being stated clearly, and to permit good communications on both sides. It is a judgment call about whether the leader should be a passive listener or an active listener, but the leader should be capable of doing both; and, when in doubt, err on the side of passive rather than active listening.

Do people fear you, distrust you, like you, respect you, love you? What do people think about you? Are they comfortable with you or are they afraid of you? Do they feel they can really tell it like it is, or do they withhold information for fear that you might explode, overreact, or make judgments about them that might be lasting and wrong? What people feel about you is important for you as a leader. If they feel good about you and if they respect and admire you, you are much more likely to have good communication with them, thereby enhancing your productivity as a leader. It is useful to remind oneself of the old adage: friends come and go, but enemies accumulate. Your spouse, children, old friends, and trusted subordinates can really help with this. Like Ed Koch, for many years the Mayor of New York City, you should ask them often: "How am I doing?"

What is your body language like? What is your office demeanor? Do you sit behind your desk and pontificate or are you willing to get away from the desk? Do you show a certain defensive nature in your body language? Are you able, literally and figuratively, to wrap your arms around people with warmth and concern? Do people feel that they can break through the interpersonal barriers that exist between subordinate and boss when discussing an issue with you? How visibly approachable are you? Many leaders are visible but not approachable and don't realize how their demeanor makes people reluctant to approach them.

Are you considered to be a communicator? Do you help your people to learn, understand, and develop? How well do you speak? Do you make brief speeches that are to the point? Do you mix humor in with your speeches? How well and how often do you write? How well do you dictate and edit?

Are you considered to be a disciplinarian? If so, are you a benign disciplinarian or a harsh disciplinarian? Do you take time to counsel people? Do you ever fire anyone? For what reasons and in what style? Do you counsel people before you relieve them of their responsibilities? Leaders who are tough, but fair, who don't confuse leniency with leadership, and who don't appear at an extreme of being too easy or too harsh, normally serve their institution well. Individuals in organizations want a leader who is a fair disciplinarian, who does not fire without careful consideration, and who sets standards for the unit that the leader also is willing to follow.

Do you enjoy your job? By letting people know that you are enjoying your job, you can help create a healthy atmosphere in your organization. Leaders who enjoy their jobs, and show everyone they do, often help their subordinates enjoy their jobs as well. Do you feel genuine joy in the successes of your subordinates?

Are you an innovator? Are you someone who hangs on to the status quo, or is caught in policy rigidities that do not allow much flexibility? General Matthew Ridgway, the great combat leader of World War II and Korea, made a very telling point after he retired from the U.S. Army: "My greatest contribution as Chief of Staff was nourishing the mavericks." Are you someone who is open to suggestions, ideas, new thoughts, new directions, and new concepts? On the other hand, are you someone who innovates too much and creates turmoil within the organization because you are constantly changing your mind on policies, organizations, personnel, and other issues? Have you the proper balance between continuity and creativity? In some situations, a great deal of innovation is needed and accepted. In other situations, innovation must be pushed slowly and incrementally to preserve the existing strength of the organization. How well do you maintain this balance?

Are you flexible? Are you an individual so rigid in your thinking and lifestyle that you are not open to ideas? Conversely, are you flexible to a fault? Do you swing with the breeze? Once you make up your mind, are you willing to stick with your decision unless strong and compelling arguments are made to change your mind? How do you fit on the continuum between too much flexibility and not enough?

Do you maintain physical and intellectual fitness? Do you show some interest in maintaining physical fitness or are you too busy or too disinclined to get involved in sporting activities or an exercise program? It is in your interest as a leader of a large organization to encourage people to have some time for physical fitness and recreation. If you are a nonathlete and you are not interested in fitness, you should, at least, consider that an athletic program may be very useful to the organization. Are you intellectually fit? Do you have a reading program? Do you bring in consultants and futurists to stretch your mind?

Are you a deflector of pressure from above or a magnifier of that pressure? One of the roles of a leader is to accept guidance and criticism in a mature way. If you are constantly magnifying the pressure that comes from your superiors and putting more and more pressure on your subordinates as a result, you may be doing a disservice to organizational morale and to your mission. At times, a leader should deflect these pressures; at other times, a leader should let some of these pressures flow through the organization.

A good rule of thumb for a leader is to be a "heat shield" for any guidance and direction from above that: (1) will do major damage to your organization's ability to accomplish its goals and/or (2) will cause serious and lasting morale problems. You probably will not be able to deflect all the heat, but you should deflect some of it.

Are you tuned in or are you out of touch? Leaders who isolate themselves in their offices or who don't have the ability to reach out and find out what's really going on, soon get a reputation for being out of touch. What are the means you use for staying tuned in? Are your antennae out all the time? Do you have good feedback mechanisms?

Are you a delegator?   There are many bosses who run their entire organization from the front office. These tend to be individuals with enormous amounts of energy and intellect. Unfortunately, such individuals do not help subordinates develop into future leaders. Leaders who often delegate authority are not only encouraging leadership at lower levels, but are also giving people a great deal of psychic reward. People who are willing to delegate rather liberally are probably doing a good job of creating a healthy organization that can carry on effectively if they should become disabled, incapacitated, or replaced by a less competent individual. A major aspect of delegation is empowerment. The top leader should empower subordinates so they have full authority to decide without checking with the top leader. Many leaders delegate conditionally when they should empower unconditionally.

One caution is in order: a leader should not be so aggressive in the desire to delegate that he or she loses touch and becomes nothing more than a traffic cop. Overdelegation can lead to the "Balkanization" of an organization, where no one is in charge.

Are you a nondrinker, a drinker, or an alcoholic?   Occasionally a leader who had a mild drinking problem prior to taking over leadership responsibilities drifts into a heavier drinking pattern that may lead to alcoholism or, at least, to a serious drinking problem. The pressures of leadership are sometimes quite severe, and individuals who have psychological or health problems relating to alcohol abuse often find their problems exacerbated. With regard to alcohol, you need to ask yourself some questions: Now that I'm a leader, what should be my approach to alcohol consumption? How am I viewed by others? The perception of alcoholism of the leader is often as important as the reality of alcoholism in the environment of a large organization.

Are you an optimist or a pessimist?   If you are constantly optimistic to the point of being a Pollyanna, and always have on your rose-colored glasses, you may lose the respect of people because you are unable to acknowledge the seamy side of your organization or to see the tough problems. On the other hand, if you are constantly pessimistic and cynical, morale in your organization can suffer. A pragmatically optimistic individual who is not a Pollyanna, but who comes to work with a lot of enthusiasm and optimism, tends to be an effective and respected leader. Although a cynic might do a good job as a leader, this cynicism and pessimism may soon transfer negatively throughout the organization.

Are you religious? What are your ethics and values?   Do you go to religious services; do you ever mention religious or moral values in your speeches or in your writings? If you attend religious services, do you ever become an active participant? When there is a funeral in your organization, are you ever asked to participate in the service? Have you ever been asked to stand up in front of a religious group and give a speech? Many people who work for you will watch you in terms of whether you are committed to a system of ethics and values. They will hope for someone as a leader who shares their values. You should be wary, however, about the danger of seeming to impose your religious standards on others. Leaders who are, or appear to be, self-righteous often fail to gain or maintain good rapport with a large number of subordinates.

Are you a writer?   Do you write a column in the weekly newspaper? How well do you write or endorse employee evaluations? Do you write letters? Do you write them well and with style? If you are a poor writer, you may unintentionally harm your people in many ways. When it is time for you to write a letter of recommendation for someone who has done an excellent job for you and the letter lacks punch, you are failing that individual. If your evaluation reports are poorly written and do not adequately highlight the performance of your subordinates, you are also doing individuals a disservice. If you are a poor writer you should get someone to help you. Get your administrative assistant, executive secretary, or your public affairs director to help you with your writing—to edit it, "clean it up," make it "punchy," make it clearer. If you learn to write well, you can better serve your organization and your efforts will be greatly appreciated. As John Kenneth Galbraith has written, "If you write well, you will automatically get attention."

Are you ambitious? Are you personally ambitious, or are you ambitious for your subordinates and your organization? In what way do your ambitions come through? A number of people who have moved to top positions in our government in recent years have been so personally ambitious that they have sometimes forgotten that a leader's first responsibility is to the mission and goals of the organization and the country.

Are you secure or are you insecure? If you are a person who is secure within, knowing your own capabilities and your own weaknesses, comfortable with yourself and with your basic lifestyle, not tending to be defensive, and able to accept criticism well, you can serve as a mature leader in many different positions. If you are basically insecure and worry a great deal about your performance and your ability to do the job, you may have a more difficult task. As you mature as a leader, your sense of security should increase as your organization succeeds. Many initially insecure people who build their self-confidence over time can become mature, successful leaders. The leader's mate can be very helpful in this regard by praising the leader's strengths and accomplishments, particularly when the leader is having problems with the organization and is not receiving much praise or support from other sources. Conversely, a mate can do much good by taking the leader down a peg or two if the leader's ego becomes overly inflated.

Are you a philanderer or a flirt? Some leaders pursue the thrills of conquest. Moral issues aside, leaders must recognize that they are being watched very carefully. If they are in business, they will be observed by their subordinates and, in some cases, by the media. If they are in government, the media often becomes an even larger factor. If they are in the military, they are being observed by their command post, security police, secretary, executive officer, and subordinates. The word quickly gets out that the boss is looking for the next liaison. Many leaders in government and politics, as well as a number in the business world and the nonprofit sectors, have seen their careers foreshortened for the simple reason that they would not control their libido.

What is your integrity level?   Leaders must realize that personal integrity and institutional integrity meet in the front office. If you have a commitment to integrity, both personal and institutional, if you talk about it, write about it, mean it, and live it, there is a good chance that institutional integrity and personal integrity throughout the organization will remain high. If, however, you are not concerned about integrity and are willing to allow the rules to be bent, institutional integrity may degenerate rapidly.

Are you an intense individual or are you relaxed?   What kind of demeanor do you project as you enter meetings, carry on conversations, and make speeches? Are you able to relax, or do the burdens and responsibilities of leadership cause you to have an intense air about you most of the time? Do you sit on the front edge of your chair? Do you interrupt people when they are trying to tell you something? These signals can help you determine your level of intensity and may help you evaluate whether your intensity adds to or detracts from your success as a leader.

Are you decisive or are you a "decision ducker"?   Some wag once said that there are three types of people: those that make things happen, those that watch things happen, and those who wonder what happened. Top leaders should follow the 60 percent rule, which states that when you have about 60 percent of the information that you need to make a decision, you should make it, because if you wait much longer to get more information you will miss some key decision points. Thus, a leader has to be both decisive and willing to make decisions without all the facts. Leaders should heed the words of Johann Schiller: "He who considers too much will perform too little."

Leaders who constantly duck decisions that should be made create an atmosphere of non-decisiveness and the organization tends to drift. Too often, decisions that should be made by the boss tend to be made by lower level people and often without full coordination. If top level decisions are always left to subordinates, many of those decisions will be very good, but consistency and coherency of policy often suffer. If you prefer to have other people within your organization make most of the decisions, you should at least ensure that there is a general consistency of policy along with full coordination.

How "conceptual" are you? Are you able to put the mission, goals, requirements, and responsibilities of your organization in a conceptual framework? Are you able to explain that conceptual framework to other people? A leader who conceptualizes well is usually a good planner and an excellent teacher.

Executive Menopause. Most leaders do not reach positions of great responsibility until they reach their 40s or early 50s. If they have climbed up the executive ladder, these leaders may have become used to working very long hours, with little time for a systematic physical exercise program, and they may have developed poor dietary habits and become heavy smokers or drinkers. Executive burnout is a rather common phenomenon for individuals of this type. This burnout can be avoided by careful time management, good control of diet and smoking, and a regular exercise program whereby vigorous exercise three or four times a week becomes an integral part of the weekly schedule. Another aspect of executive menopause is the tendency of some leaders to be seduced by "perks." Company airplanes, free homes, magnificent offices, superb outer office support, opportunities to travel widely, can all, in an insidious way, divert the attention of the leader from the mission.

When considering military leadership, J.F.C. Fuller's classic small book, *Generalship: Its Diseases and Their Cures*, makes

the point that the best generalship in war occurs in leaders between the ages of thirty-four and forty-five because combat
leadership requires the physical strength, courage, stamina,
flexibility, and risk-taking more often found in younger men
and seldom found in men past the age of fifty. He examined 100
great military leaders of history and found that at the time of
their greatest triumph they tended to be quite young (74 percent were forty-five or younger). Although Fuller's book was
written before World War II, it seems to support the present
personnel philosophy of the United States military, which has
most senior officers retiring in their early fifties.

Avoiding both the Peter and the Paul Principles. Leaders can avoid
the Peter Principle by proper preparation for each higher level
of responsibility. The Paul Principle can also be avoided
through hard work and good planning.

The Peter Principle, whereby individuals tend to get promoted to their "level of incompetence" and then get stuck
there, is commonly understood. Leaders should be careful to
avoid the Peter Principle themselves, and to do their best to
prevent it from becoming the norm in the organizations they
lead. Promotion systems should concentrate heavily on *potential* and should be flexible enough so that when it is clear that
people have reached their "level of incompetence," steps can be
taken to gently move them back to a level where they can function effectively.

The Paul Principle is less well understood, but it can be
almost as destructive to good leadership as the Peter Principle.
The Paul Principle is the gradual obsolescence of leaders as
they lose touch with the organization they lead, become too
conservative, resist innovation and change, and fail to take advantage of technological breakthroughs. A systematic reading
program, participation in management training symposia or
workshops, regular interaction with long-range planners, and
brainstorming activities with the staff can all help to keep executives from falling into this insidious trap.

One of the ways that a president of a major corporation
whom I interviewed keeps up with changing technology is

through the use of an up-to-date personal computer in his home. He keeps the latest Macintosh model on his desk and uses it for correspondence and record-keeping. He even plays an occasional game on the computer. He favors games that are very mind-stretching in terms of the use of sophisticated software; these games are also fun.

When I lecture on leadership and discuss the Paul Principle I say something like: "Too many top leaders are brain dead." This comment almost always gets a laugh and some knowing nods. Why? Because it is fundamentally true; too many executives let their brains rest when they should be using them actively and at their full potential. The Paul Principle can be overcome by leaders with the kind of energetic commitment to creativity and innovation that they exhibited on the way to the top. If, as a top executive, you are bored, tired, or looking forward to retirement, you should accelerate that decision—retire next month and let someone else take the reins! Just because you worked long and hard to reach the top doesn't mean that the company owes you a number of years in semi-retirement as CEO. If you are burned-out, admit it and take early retirement. It is much better for you and the enterprise that you lead to leave a year too early rather than a year (or two or more) too late.

A related problem is the "last-year syndrome." Unhappily, many executives become bitter, cynical, and imperious during the last year at the top. This can be caused by a number of factors: the realization that all the goals that they had set for their organization will not be met, the understanding that they soon will give up all the trappings of power, the fear of the unknowns of retirement life, the anticipation of withdrawal pains, the realization that age has crept up on them. As a leader approaches the one-year point, he or she should make a concerted effort to avoid the last-year syndrome. In some cases, the leader should decide to retire a year early and give the new team a chance to take charge.

The Red Reactor Problem.   Those leaders who react emotionally or violently to criticism from below often fail as leaders because, over time, they lose touch with the organizations they are charged to lead. They also tend to lose some of their best subordinates who, out of frustration, move on to other places where constructive criticism and healthy debate are part of the organizational climate. Leaders who take criticism poorly damage vital feedback mechanisms and may cause subordinates to jump ship. When such leaders face crises, they will look futilely for the creative subordinate who could have bailed them out. Over time, such leaders also have difficulty recruiting talented individuals, for the word quickly spreads that the top leader is unreceptive to criticism. A particularly unfortunate quality in a leader is a combination of poor reaction to criticism and a tendency to hold grudges. Those individuals who know they are "Red Reactors" and who receive criticism poorly should strive to constrain this personality preference; at the same time, they should look for individuals with enough self-confidence not to be intimidated by an occasional outburst from the leader.

Knowing your people.   How many people within a large organization should a leader know personally? A good, general rule of thumb is 500. Leaders should know their immediate staff, their key subordinates, and the immediate subordinates of all of the key subordinates. Added together, this number is likely to be between 50 and 100. Executives should also know a good number of people in the field offices, on the production line, in the legal office, in the financial office, in the marketing offices, etc. The leader should know important informal leaders, especially in the various minority groups. Employees who are particularly outstanding or particularly troublesome should be known by the top executive. The executive may wish to give each group some personal attention at various times. If the leader knows more than 500 employees he or she may be spending too much time learning (and retaining) names and too little time focusing on the important issues. If, on the other hand, the leader knows fewer than 200 individuals, he or she may be losing touch with the people who can provide valuable information, ideas, and insights.

"Do it all" leaders burn themselves out; "delegate it all" leaders lose touch; "sliders" postpone too many decisions; "hyperambitious" leaders spend too much time impressing the boss and depressing their followers. Wise leaders avoid these pitfalls through introspection.

If, after going through the exercise of careful introspection, you decide that leadership of large organizations is not your bag, it is best to begin to make preparation for other work. People who don't find leadership an uplifting and rewarding experience should not seek big leadership jobs or stay in them if they are at the top. Introspection can help you decide if you can march with enthusiasm to the beat of the leadership drum.

14

DEALING WITH THE MEDIA

the challenge and the opportunity

Just because you are not paranoid doesn't mean that people aren't out to get you.

—*Robert Pfaltzgraff*

Truth is generally the best vindication against slander.

—*Abraham Lincoln*

Meeting the press fairly and squarely is a challenge of considerable proportions for leaders. Those leaders who make it a policy to avoid contact with the media, except as a last resort, miss the chance to learn and grow in the crucible of challenge and response that an active free press provides in democratic systems.

Even more importantly, the media can provide an opportunity for a leader to compliment and thank others, and to get proper recognition for the organization and its people. Therefore, the leader should seek out the media and try to bring them in to write stories and produce television shows or clips in support of the organization's goals and to highlight the accomplishments of individuals. Leaders should not take the attitude that the media is the enemy, that the press cannot be trusted, or that the best policy is to avoid any contact with reporters. In general, the media can be helpful. It is important, though, to maintain an attitude of skepticism because you may periodically be burned by some members of the media, whether you call them in or not. It is important to be accurate in what you say to journalists and to avoid making statements that can be easily taken out of context or misquoted.

It is useful to establish ground rules in each contact with the media. Will this interview be on or off the record? Will you have the opportunity to see the manuscript or the videotape before it goes final? If not, why not? It is generally useful to speak informally with the reporter before you get into the formal interview to find out whether that reporter has any major preconceptions or misconceptions. If so, you can try to correct or rectify these. If you cannot, you should be particularly wary of what you say because, when media representatives have already made up their minds, it is often a question of trying to "limit damage" as much as possible. If a member of the media is clearly biased and is not likely to do a fair story, you have a responsibility to alert your bosses and the public affairs people at higher levels to let them know that a critical article or program will soon appear despite your best efforts.

If a reporter is willing to show the manuscript to you before it goes to press, you may clear up some misconceptions, correct errors that might have been made, help expand some points that need expanding, and so forth. Many responsible journalists will allow you to help them if you have established a sense of mutual respect and an understanding of the importance of telling the story correctly and accurately. Joking with the media, relaxing with them, giving them the opportunity to observe firsthand what your organization does, giving them the chance to see some things that they would not normally see and to talk to people with whom they would not normally have contact, are some useful techniques to consider. These techniques can ensure an accurate media insight into your organization and establish appropriate rapport with the influential news profession, breaking down the natural barriers that often exist.

When a media visit is imminent, a leader can run stories in the company or installation newspaper telling the readers that ABC News or the *New York Times* or the *Economist* is coming to do a story. The leader can explain that the media's interest is a compliment. The presence of the media can be used as a motivating and uplifting experience for members of your unit. If you can get the story out ahead of time, you can show the members of the press that you have, in fact, alerted your subordinates that they are coming, that you are happy that they are there, and that you have encouraged candor in answering their questions. You may consequently establish a good rapport between working members of the press and yourself which can carry on for years.

Often, when members of the media ask questions of a leader, they don't ask the best questions. If you feel comfortable in dealing with members of the media who are asking the questions, you can often steer them in the right direction. If the interviewer asks a question that is not particularly relevant, you can answer the question but follow up with, "That was a good question, but I think there is a better question that you might have asked along the following lines." Then you ask the question and answer it yourself. This will educate the media representative, and it is to be hoped that he or she will pick up on your points. The interview can thus become more productive. Members of the media often spread themselves so thin across so many issues and so many places that they really don't know what questions to ask. You can help them ask the right questions. This technique can put you in charge of the interview and help to tell the story you want to tell.

Leaders should have an agenda, a point of view or theme, that they want to get across during the interview. They should answer the questions in such a way that the agenda comes across loud and clear. There is a story about Donald Rumsfeld when he was Secretary of Defense that illustrates this point. Rumsfeld was asked in a press interview how his elderly mother was. Rumsfeld's reply was that she was fine but that she was worried about the Soviet threat!

Members of the media are looking for a news hook: something interesting to hang the story on. A leader can help provide this hook if he or she is sensitive to the needs of the press and reaches out to his or her staff and subordinates to get ideas on how to bring something newsworthy to the attention of the reporter.

A leader can use upcoming news conferences as a means to force subordinates to come up with recommended courses of action. For instance, President Kennedy used his biweekly press conference to accelerate the decisionmaking process, to keep informed on current issues, and to make policy decisions. In addition, speechwriters can be useful instruments in the decisionmaking process. In fact, official speeches are often the most important means by which decisions are announced. Leaders should ensure that there is a close relationship between their speechwriters and their public affairs specialists (as well as between those two groups and the key officials throughout the organization) so that interactions with the media and the general public can be as positive as possible.

Some large organizations have a media-training program for senior executives that gives them a chance to face various media opportunities in a well-simulated environment. In this training, the one-on-one interview, the general news conference, the confrontational news conference, the remote interview, and the speech followed by a question-and-answer format are all videotaped. The executive is then critiqued on style, body language, sense of humor, speaking voice, etc. Individuals who expect to move into top executive positions should take this training.

Although some have argued that America has developed into a massive adversary culture where disparagement by the media of all our institutions has become the norm, mature leaders can find ways to work positively with representatives of the news profession. Leaders of large organizations cannot hide from media representatives; they should stay in close touch with their public affairs officers and seek their guidance and support often.

Finally and perhaps most importantly, an executive must ask himself or herself honestly how firmly committed he or she is to freedom of the press and a robust first amendment. The leader who loves to be secretive, who feels the media is not a responsible element in society, or who is uncomfortable in his or her interrelationship with members of the press, is likely to be treated unfairly by the media. This unfair treatment is often a result of a member of the press feeling frustrated in the desire to have a full dialogue with the executive. On being thwarted by the reluctance of the executive to be open, candid, and helpful, the reporter sometimes takes out frustrations by writing a critical and unfair article. It is clear that leaders of large organizations in all areas of society must realize that they will have some media attention and must conduct their personal and professional lives with that fact in mind.

15

CREATING A STRATEGIC VISION

the role of planning

The basis of individual and national progress is the willingness to sacrifice the present for the future. That is the way nations get ahead and that is the way individuals get ahead.

—William Feather

Where there is no vision, the people perish.

—Proverbs XXIX, 18

The great leaders of our time have been not only effective operators and decisionmakers, but also people of vision who have had a marvelous sense of what was possible, how to set and articulate goals, and how to motivate their people to strive successfully for these goals. Great leaders tend to be great planners.

Having served in a number of key planning positions in government and having written two books and a number of articles on strategic planning, I have come to the conclusion that systematic planning in the American cultural environment is quite difficult. One of the major problems is that individuals within large organizations often view planning from very different perspectives. Senior executives must understand that planning in the budget office is quite different from planning in operational divisions, or from planning in the personnel or manpower directorates. It is the task of the leader to establish a planning system that allows specialized planning to take place, but always within the context of a strategic planning system.

There are several important rules regarding the relationship between the leader and the planning staff at the corporate, agency, or service headquarters. First, the leader must have direct access to the planners and should schedule time on a regular basis to meet with them. The leader must read, know, and understand the organization's most significant plans. Lastly, the leader has to be willing to exercise operational plans periodically to allow the organization to practice important elements of these plans.

All large organizations should prepare a long-range plan and update it annually. Leaders should find time to meet every month or so with their long-range planner (or planners), so that they can gain exposure to the frontiers of developments in technology, marketing techniques, and management concepts, as well as to changing trends in national and international economics.

The annual long-range plan should be brief, usually about ten to twelve pages. It should be signed by the top leader and should be distributed widely throughout the organization (though it may require a classified supplement to ensure that competitors and others do not have full access to some aspects of the plan). The leader should refer to this plan periodically throughout the year. (Calling it "our strategic plan" is a useful technique.) Key subordinates should be assured that the leader will make decisions based on the strategic vision outlined in the long-range plan. If an organization has a strategic vision that includes specific goals and priorities developed in the long-range plan, day-to-day decisionmaking is much more likely to have real coherence. Goals can charge up people, can ignite the human spirit. If goals are carefully constructed and well understood, and if they enhance the successful accomplishment of the mission, both good and bad luck can be better managed.

Executives should understand that a strategic plan has important symbolic value. Even if you may not wish to take any major new initiatives in the near term, many subordinates want, need, and expect some kind of strategic vision for their organization; the strategic plan can accomplish this.

Another important element of planning is divestiture planning. All large organizations need to aggressively pursue divestiture strategies to ensure that they do not retain outdated or outmoded policies, offices, doctrines, or research and development programs. Divestiture planning in business is normally easier to accomplish than divestiture planning in government. Economic analysis in a profitmaking firm normally points to areas of weakness and obsolescence within the organization. In government, divestiture is a more difficult process because the obsolete areas are harder to identify and more difficult to exorcise from the organization. The long-range planners can help in this regard by laying out an overall structure for the organization twenty years into the future. This helps the leader focus attention on areas that will not be relevant by the year 2010, 2015, 2020, etc. By working in close coordination with long-range planners and a divestiture team, the leader can develop a scheme for phasing out those elements of the organization which should not be present two decades hence. Divestiture should ideally take place before obsolescence sets in, before the organization, system, or doctrine is in decline. Preemptive divestiture should be the goal so that buggy whips, candle factories, "coast artillery cannon" and "horse cavalries" of the future are phased out much more promptly than they were in the past. Divestiture teams must be carefully protected by the top leader. Many field agency and staff officials resent individuals who recommend initiatives for divestiture. Divestiture often means loss of jobs, power, and prestige.

The executive should adhere to the "dignified burial" rule of thumb and spend a considerable portion of his or her time and energy helping the employees find new and exciting opportunities in the firm, if at all possible. Other employees will be watching how you manage the divestiture process, and if you accomplish it ruthlessly and with little consideration for their fellow workers who are affected, this action could have a negative impact on the morale of the entire organization.

A good example of creative divestiture was shared with

me by a CEO of a large newspaper chain. Because of the very rapidly changing technological situation in the publishing business, he decided to form a small software team to design a better system to get reporters' stories into print. The team came up with a very innovative way to use and internet personal computers. The system not only saved a lot of time and money, but also was very popular with the reporters. A number of other newspapers and publishing firms learned of this new system and started to buy the software packages that his team had designed. For a brief period of time the publisher considered going into the software business, but then decided that he wanted to stay true to his strategic plan of remaining within the boundaries of a communications company. Hence, he sold off his software business at a considerable profit.

No matter what business a company is in, it is often useful for leaders to ask themselves periodically if the company is staying within the context of what it knows how to do and what it has established as its overall framework. When a company wanders too far from its field of expertise it often gets into serious trouble. The example of LTV comes to mind. A very successful and highly respected aerospace company, LTV expanded into the steel making and truck making business. The result: bankruptcy, which has not only damaged the company seriously but also has hurt a very large number of pensioners. Successful CEOs should avoid the tendency to assume that just because they can run a firm well they can run anything well. Technical competence in the company's major endeavors is an important attribute for the top leader. If he or she doesn't have it, the likelihood of failure increases.

Hence, divestiture is not just unloading the "dogs," it is also selling off parts of the business that do not fit within the corporate "essence." There are similar situations in government and the military. For instance, General Marshall was very wise to support an autonomous, separate United States Air Force so the Army could concentrate in the post-World-War-II period on its essence, ground combat.

As a new leader takes over a large organization, two of the most important questions are: "What is the long-range plan?"

and "Who are the long-range planners?" If planners do not have direct access to you as a leader, reorganize to ensure that they do. If a leader of a large organization is not committed to an institutionalized planning process, the leader is likely to become merely a caretaker who is unable to raise the organization to higher levels of performance in pursuit of important goals. Leaders should remember Lincoln's insight, "A mind stretched by a new idea never returns to its original dimension." Long-range planners can and should stretch the mind of the leader and they should do so regularly.

The long-range planning division with direct access to both the chief executive officer and the other top officials in both the corporate headquarters and the field agencies can be a marvelous clearinghouse for ideas.

One of the great problem areas that all leaders face is a reluctance to develop a mindset that requires spending considerable time planning for a period beyond the leader's expected tenure. This is an acute problem in federal and state government, where many leaders expect to retain their positions for no more than four years. These restricted time horizons are a great detriment to a long-range planning process, which should impact on day-to-day decisions.

A major goal of a planning system is to encourage creativity and innovation throughout the organization. Many leaders give lip service to innovation while, at the same time, they fail to create either the climate or the organizational structure to encourage innovation. Leaders should periodically examine the quality, quantity, and velocity of innovation within their organization. They should ask how each new idea furthers the mission of the organization. They should be open to new ideas while being sensitive to the turbulence that the implementation of new ideas can often cause.

The velocity of innovation has two components: the speed and ease by which new ideas can reach the top level leaders, and the speed and ease of the process whereby the new idea is implemented throughout the organization. Leaders should periodically measure these two aspects of the velocity of innovation; auditors and inspection teams can assist them in this assessment. A leader should look for ways to increase the velocity of innovation. Many leaders tolerate organizational structures which make the movement of new ideas from originator to key decisionmakers both slow and difficult. Many large organizations are like a long corridor with dozens of doors in a row. If any of the doors is locked, the idea dies. The leader must not only reduce the number of doors; he or she must also ensure that many people have keys to the doors that remain.

The Model Installation Program of the Department of Defense provides a useful example of both innovation and organizational autonomy that is worth examining. The program, which, so far has been a great success, gives the post or base commander the opportunity to make decisions on his or her own in order to operate more efficiently and effectively. He or she is able to keep the money he or she saves and use it largely as he or she chooses to improve the operation of the post or base. In the past, such savings were returned to the Federal Treasury. This arrangement provided little incentive to base or post officials to actively seek improvements. The Model Installation Program has many more people actively looking for efficiencies in order to generate funds for badly needed improvements. The substance and velocity of innovation has decidedly improved as a result of this imaginative DOD program. A similar program could have wide applicability in the business world.

Part of the planning process is taking a long-range view of the organizational structure to ensure that as goals, priorities, technology, and the workforce change the organization changes to meet the new opportunities and challenges. There is a tendency for executives to err in one of two directions. On the one side, some leaders and institutions love to reorganize and do so too often. This causes unnecessary disruption and turbulence within their organizations (and, at times, within neighboring and supporting organizations). The best example I know in this regard is the United States Army. The turbulence that results because of constant restructuring not only hurts the Army but confuses the other military services that must work with and support the Army. Leaders who have a tendency to reorganize often should heed the sage advice of Norm Augustine, who wrote, "Remember: New Tree, Same Monkeys."

The error on the other side is more common: the failure of the leaders to anticipate the need for organizational change as they carry out their various plans and initiatives. A close friend who is a CEO of a large privately held corporation aggressively acquired a number of companies in a four-year period. He soon found himself in a situation where his president had seventeen general managers reporting to him, where four years before he had had only eight. After about a year in which his president was so busy that he barely had time to return the crisis-type phone calls, the CEO reorganized and placed a number of the smaller units of his expanded company under a district manager. The president's span of control was significantly decreased and the company flourished. An executive who is a good planner will make reorganization part of his or her acquisition strategy, so as he or she acquires more companies (or, conversely, divests himself of companies), the organization will be ready to handle the new realities.

Some planning is good; some is bad. There is, however, an unfortunate tendency in this country for many individuals in business and in government to be skeptical of long-range planning. The many failures in the Soviet Union and Eastern Europe that seem to be a direct result of poor long-range planning often are cited as examples of why planning is a mistake. It is certainly clear that the ideologically based planning systems in the totalitarian socialist states have been colossal failures, but these failures should not discourage leaders in democratic states from doing long-range planning.

The long-term planning done by some of the pharmaceutical and biotechnology companies, as they identified major medical needs (anti-cholesterol drugs, blood clot destroyers, etc.), committed significant research and development resources, and consequently developed drugs of major health-saving and economic importance, is an example of the dramatic success that can result from long-range planning.

All planning systems can become too rigid and out of

touch with reality, but a leader who is a flexible planner and who has a vision based on careful thought and research can lead the organization to new heights of performance and effectiveness. Conversely, a leader who, for ideological (or any other) reasons, rejects planning, misses opportunities. A combination of good systematic planning and flexible "ad-hocracy" can lead to extraordinary results.

As leaders communicate with their followers in meetings, with speeches, and through newsletters and newspapers, they can help their organizations keep a commitment to long-range planning. To use my favorite phrase in this regard: "I am interested in the future because that's where I plan to spend the rest of my life."

16

LEADING INTERNATIONAL ORGANIZATIONS

dealing with cultural complexities and national antagonisms

Sometimes a man's fitness for a post of trust is determined by his associations.

—Sidney Hook

Leadership of international corporations and multinational government organizations is a particularly demanding responsibility. The leader should understand and be sensitive to cultural differences, national biases, antagonisms between and among national groups, unusual administrative and bureaucratic processes, and so forth. When an individual is going to move into a new situation involving the supervision of people from a number of nations, it is useful to do some background reading on each of those nations. For example, books by authors like Anthony Samson on England, Luigi Barzini on Italy, Gordon Craig on Germany, and Edwin Reischauer on Japan are available. Individuals from the various nations are enormously complimented when their boss is able to speak knowledgeably about their history and their traditions; the earlier the reading is done, the better.

Many large corporations have become truly international and the employees, particularly the younger ones, think of themselves as international people with no strong ties to an

individual nation. They become very mobile, are often proficient in two or more languages, and sometimes marry individuals from nations other than their own. These trends are generally favorable to the top leadership of these companies, for it is
easier to move these people around than to move those with
strong emotional ties to an individual country. In addition, this
trend is helpful because decisions sometimes must be made that
may not be in the national interest of particular countries. If the
top corporate officers are too closely associated with an individual nation, they may not be able to make decisions as objectively as they should in serving their stockholders. This trend,
however, is not without its problems. The host nation of the
corporate headquarters may take a strong position on an issue
that may make the corporate officers quite uncomfortable.
Whether it be trade with South Africa, war with one or more
countries, national conscription, or reserve military duty, the
corporate officers are sometimes faced with a set of bad choices
to pick from. Similarly, government leaders must take into account the delicate position that multinational corporations face
as they try to carry out their corporate decisions.

In every international organization there will always be
some cross-national antagonisms with which the leader must
deal. In my two years' experience of leading individuals from
five nations (Great Britain, Germany, Belgium, the Netherlands,
and the United States), I found that severe cross-national antagonisms existed. For instance, a few weeks after I moved into
the organization, I asked a Dutch lieutenant colonel if he
spelled his first name (Frans) with an "s" or a "z." With considerable anger, he replied that the Germans spelled it with a "z."

If I had done my research, I would not have asked the
question, for I would have known not only the answer, but also
the Dutch-German sensitivities. Another example of the mani-
festation of this antagonism was my German boss who asked
me to act as the disciplinarian for any Dutch or Belgian subordinate who needed counselling. As the German pointed out to
me, "Everyone likes Americans, but some people don't like
Germans."

In many cases, there are work-ethic differentials between

and among the nations in international organizations. These differences cause morale problems on both sides. Individuals from nations that are accustomed to working short hours and taking long lunch breaks tend to be critical of those who work longer and harder, and vice versa. It is important for the leader to establish a standard for work hours and ensure that the standard is followed. Generally, the standard should be a compromise between the various extremes. For instance, Americans tend to work long hours and to be quite concerned about deadlines. Europeans, on the other hand, tend to work less frenetically; they spend more time on the bigger issues and less time on the minutiae.

Language difficulties are very common in international organizations. As a result, the individuals that speak and write the language of the organization have both a great advantage and a great burden. If English is the language of the organization, as is commonly the case, then the British, the Americans, the Canadians, and other English speakers (the Germans, Dutch, and Scandinavians also tend to be quite proficient in English) will be expected to do most of the work: the writing, the speaking, and the briefing. On the other hand, the leader must ensure that individuals who do not speak and write English as well are not removed from the decisionmaking process and are not neglected in staff activities. This is a very delicate issue. For instance, if they are given only the easy or noncontroversial actions, the leader will soon face a morale problem because those individuals will feel they are being cut out of the important issues and actions.

Although not normally a problem in business, in a governmental setting there may be large differences in pay and allowances of employees that the leader will have to deal with. There may be civil servants and military officers working side by side with the same ranks or grade levels but with major pay differentials (as much as 100 percent). There is very little that the leader can do about this, but as activities are planned that require individuals to commit their personal funds (parties, receptions, and picnics), it is important for the leader to be very sensitive to the fact that some people are not as well paid as others.

Within every multinational governmental organization, there will be people from nations that are large, rich, and powerful and others from nations that are smaller, poorer, and less powerful. The "small nation syndrome" must be understood by the leader. Representatives from small nations must be treated with care and substantive meetings should include representatives from all nations, even though the issue may have very little to do with one or two of the smaller nations. These nations deserve "a seat at the table," and the leader must ensure that they always have one, for each individual represents a sovereign state despite differences in size or power.

Americans often become "bulls in china shops" when they join an international organization. The "American way" of dealing with problems sometimes fails in the international milieu. It is particularly important for American leaders of international organizations to be sensitive to national concerns and to listen carefully to their advisers from other nations.

The transition process is important as well when you are about to take over an international organization. You should ensure that the initial briefings are given, to a large extent, by individuals from nations other than your own. Your outer office should include secretaries, executive assistants, protocol officials, and public affairs and community relations specialists from various nations.

In the course of day-to-day business, leaders of large international organizations should spend the great majority of their time with colleagues from other nations rather than with their compatriots. This approach is important from the point of view of both substance and perception.

Would-be leaders in international corporations should try to obtain positions that will enhance their understanding of other cultures as they move up in the company. Overseas experience, language competence, and cultural sophistication can be very helpful when you become a leader of a large international organization; with these assets, you can reach out to people of many nations.

17

SPOUSES OF THE LEADERSHIP TEAM
the delicate balance

One of the best hearing aids a man can have is an attentive wife.

—Groucho Marx

One of the more sensitive issues that leaders face in the current cultural environment is that of the spouse in a supporting role. In some leadership situations, the spouse of the leader has a very small role to play, but in many others, the role can be and is quite important. Many spouses of leaders play a productive role as a quiet supporter, critic, conduit for information, and sounding board. The role that Prince Philip plays in supporting Queen Elizabeth in her many substantive and ceremonial roles, or the role that Eleanor Roosevelt played in supporting her husband while making a real difference in some independent areas, can be emulated with good results by spouses of leaders in many organizational settings.

When the spouse begins to be perceived as being involved in policy issues, the hiring and firing of key subordinates, etc., the impact on the effectiveness and morale of the organization can be significant. The leader should be sensitive to these concerns and should not allow the spouse, no matter how strong the personality, to influence policy. There have been many interesting case studies in the American political and economic system that seem to indicate the dangers of a spouse exercising an inordinate amount of power and influence. Such cases as Phillip Agee and Mary Cunningham at Bendix in the early 1980s and the role of the President's wife in the Wilson, Harding, and Carter Presidencies bring to mind the inherent dangers to the credibility of the leader with a spouse whose influence extends well past the family circle.

Another sensitive issue, for many, is the role that spouses of members of the top leadership team play in supporting the activities of the organization. This subject can be fraught with so much emotion and residual hard feelings that some leaders prefer not to discuss it or outline a policy position, either formal or informal, on the subject.

From my experience in leading both line and staff organizations, and as a head of an academic institution, I have come to the conclusion that spouses of subordinate leaders should never be pressured to participate in activities that support the organization. However, those who choose to participate should be given full latitude to do so and should be thanked and thanked often for their willingness to be helpful. Perhaps a few examples will help illustrate my point.

A research company that has grown at a rate of 60 percent per year since it was started eight years ago has five major groups, each under a vice president. The Chairman of the Board has noticed that one of the groups has a very active social program led by the spouse of the vice president. Another group has no social program at all, and the other groups are somewhere in between. The group with the active social program has the lowest turnover rate and the highest productivity rate. Recently the employees and the spouses of this group pulled together, on a volunteer basis, to help an individual in the group with a severe health problem—in a way that not only helped the individual, but also helped draw attention to a little-known health problem that needed national attention. The entire organization took pride in the fact that the company was willing to be so helpful to someone in need.

This Chairman of the Board has a definite philosophy regarding the social and supportive activities of the spouses in the various elements of his company. He never puts pressure on the subordinate leader or the spouse who does nothing in this area, but he *privately* thanks the subordinate leader and the spouse who have such an active program. He has noticed that the other groups that are doing more in this area seem to be doing so because of the "emulation effect." He feels that it would be a mistake to encourage other vice presidents to do more and is quite satisfied to see informal emulation take place.

Another example may be useful. At military bases overseas there are lots of young wives of military men who need support and assistance. Some of these young women, many still in their teens, are homesick, unable to find work because of restrictive laws of the host country, living far away from the post without transportation, or living in very substandard housing because of the weakness of the dollar and the low pay of the junior enlisted members of the armed services. The military can and does give some official support for these spouses, but it is often inadequate. This is where the spouses of the leadership team can really help out if they are willing to come forward and volunteer their time, energy, and creativity to build and sustain programs to assist.

The natural tendency to reach out and help people in need is often sufficient and the only real requirement for the spouses of the key leaders is to show interest and support for the activities that are already underway. However, in certain cases this informal, volunteer support structure does not exist or is so inadequate that the real needs are not being met. In this case, the leader is faced with a difficult dilemma. Subordinates are making strong, legitimate complaints that something must be done and that other posts and bases are doing a much better job of supporting families in need. If the leader's spouse is able and willing, he or she can provide the leadership in forming groups and recruiting volunteers to assist. If the leader has no spouse, or if the spouse is unable or unwilling to provide that leadership, the issue becomes even more delicate. The leader must reach out and find someone else's spouse who is willing to lead the effort in building this voluntary support structure. The leader can do this in a number of ways. He or she can raise the issue in a staff meeting, write an editorial in the weekly newspaper, or talk about the problem at various social gatherings. The art of gentle persuasion rather than the use of influence or pressure should be the guideline here. Once the willing spouse or spouses come forward, the top leader has to be willing to provide time on the calendar to interact actively with these volunteers, to listen to ideas and feedback, and to give guidance and support.

One of the big mistakes a leader can make is to put heavy pressure on the spouses of key subordinates to participate in these programs. Many spouses will resent this pressure, while some will feel guilty about not properly supporting their spouse's careers. The result can be very poor morale among the top leadership group. The leader should avoid the word "expect" when asking the support of spouses of subordinates. For instance, the seemingly benign appeal "I realize that many of your spouses are busy working, raising families, and participating in volunteer activities outside the organizational environment, but I expect them to assist as much as they can," can be devastating or insulting to some spouses. The word "expect" can be a very "heavy" term in this context. Many spouses will interpret this to mean that if they can't give a certain number of hours each week to these activities their spouse's career will be damaged. Some leaders make the mistake of establishing policy that every spouse of every subordinate leader must get involved in activities that support the organization. The rationale is often "if everyone doesn't contribute, those that do will have to do more." This rationale fails to take into account the voluntary nature of spouse activities. In addition, it is hopelessly out of date.

Heaps of private and/or public praise for those who help, a willingness to accept an informal support structure that may not be as strong as it might have been twenty or thirty years ago, and a resistance to the temptation to pressure spouses should be the ground rules for leaders. I have seen leaders fail badly with the best intentions at heart when they or their spouses (or both) violated these ground rules. Through heavy pressure they have built up impressive spouse support structures, but they have, in so doing, destroyed the morale of the top leadership group and done damage to the institution itself.

The leader should try to put himself or herself in the position of the spouse of the subordinate. The spouse badly wants his or her husband or wife to be happy and successful. But he or she may have a very rewarding career that prevents heavy involvement in activities outside his or her own job environment. Or the subordinate's spouse may be deeply committed to family, church, or charity efforts that are outside the context of your organization. Pressure from the big boss concerning spouse involvement can exact a heavy emotional penalty from the entire family of the subordinate, and over time may damage the performance of the subordinate leader. The leader should also be sensitive to the dangers of his or her spouse going on a "power trip" and making active involvement of spouses of subordinates in volunteer activities a "loyalty check." The worst example of this I ever observed personally was a colonel's wife in Europe who would, on occasion, tell a young wife of a junior officer, "I'll have your husband's job," if she didn't participate in some activity.

In organizations where social service volunteer activities play a key role and the number of true volunteers is diminishing, the senior leader has to make an estimate of the situation and see what the real options are. If he or she is not careful, a heavy load will fall on a small group of perennial volunteers who eventually wind up burned out and disillusioned. There have been instances where a simple explanation of the need for volunteers, combined with a creative support system (such as free transportation to and from the home and on the job), has resulted in a large number of volunteers coming forth.

If the support structure is needed and the voluntary structure will not meet these needs, the top leader should consider funding a support effort with company funds.

One technique that the World Bank uses to reward spouses for their patience and support is a point system. For every night that an official of the bank spends away from home a point is awarded. After a certain number of points are earned, the spouse can travel with the employee at the expense of the World Bank. Hence when the employee does travel the spouse knows that points are being earned and particularly attractive trips together can be looked forward to.

The supportive spouse is not always a wife. By serving as a sounding board, a source of quiet advice, a caring critic, and a source of direct feedback, the husband of a female leader can be an equally effective supporter. Fine models of recent times would be the husbands of British Prime Minister Margaret Thatcher and of Jeane Kirkpatrick, the former U.S. Representative to the United Nations.

18

ESTABLISHING STANDARDS

personal and institutional integrity

There is no pillow so soft as a clear conscience.

—French Proverb

God brings men into deep waters, not to drown them but to cleanse them.

—Aughery

Upon assumption of the leadership of an organization, it is important for the executive to make clear the standards of integrity that are to be adhered to by the organization. One way to do that is through the company newspaper or a newsletter, where the leader can write down precisely what he or she means by integrity and what standards are to be established and maintained. The new leader should also talk about integrity in shop get-togethers, in staff meetings, with subordinate leaders, and so forth. In the process of writing and talking about integrity, the leader should use examples from personal experience.

Early in your tenure you should look for opportunities to demonstrate, within the context of the organization which you now lead, your commitment to integrity. Perhaps a brief personal example will best illustrate this point. At Bitburg, Germany, we were conducting a NATO air defense exercise and my intelligence officer got up in front of all the pilots to outline the reporting guidelines. He said he wanted the pilots to report that they had expended four missiles and half of the rounds from the Gatling gun. He also wanted each pilot to report that he had shot down four enemy aircraft. I interrupted the intelligence officer because of my concern about these ground rules. I said to the assembled group: "We will not do that; I don't want to set an example, even in an exercise, of dishonest reporting. What I want you to do is go up, intercept the inbound aggressor airplanes, make your simulated attacks, and report what you actually accomplish. If you shoot down four airplanes in simulated combat, report four airplanes. If you shoot down no airplanes, report no airplanes. Don't falsify reports just to exercise the system." It was a fine opportunity to demonstrate that we would not set a pattern of prevarication in our day-to-day activities, but that we would report honestly and fairly what we did.

Another true story also illustrates my point about personal integrity. Babe Didrikson-Zaharias was a great athlete in the 1932 Olympics and later became a professional golfer. While playing in a tournament on the golf tour she noticed she had somehow played the wrong ball. When the round was over she penalized herself two strokes, which cost her first place in the tournament. Later, in a quiet conversation, one of her friends asked her, "Babe, why did you do that? No one would have known that you used the wrong ball." Babe answered, "Don't you understand—*I* would have known."

It is this kind of personal integrity we need to emphasize in all institutions and organizations in our country—a personal commitment to integrity that is deep and profound. In combination with a strong commitment to institutional or corporate integrity, this personal strength of character is what leaders should stress and stress frequently. There are people who would never lie in their personal lives but who would lie for their institution. Yet institutional integrity is just as important and, in some cases, more important than personal integrity, although they are inseparable. Low levels of institutional integrity damage the credibility of the organization, your own credibility, personal trust, and mutual respect.

Another aspect of integrity that leaders should consider is "protecting their signature." Since most of the letters, memoranda, staff papers, messages, regulations, and directives that they sign will be prepared by members of their staff, they should do an "integrity check" before they sign the paper. From my experience the most common violation of integrity is in the personnel system. The general who states that "this is the best lieutenant colonel working for me" can only do this about once a year, or he undermines his credibility within the personnel and promotion system. There is a great irony in this area. By pushing too many people too hard, the leader hurts them all because his or her signature and endorsement lose value and, in fact, sometimes become a negative factor.

Part of personal integrity is to avoid artificially inflating the importance of one's organization or one's self. People who build empires beyond that which the mission requires not only are making a mistake, in a fundamental sense, but may also be violating their integrity by misleading their bosses or their shareholders.

An insidious, but very common, breach of integrity occurs when subordinates are excessively burdened with the task of reporting trivial accomplishments. Often subordinates will certify the accomplishment of something without actually doing the work. They justify this violation of integrity by saying "no one will know and no one will care" or "this is a dumb requirement." A useful approach is to initiate action to change the requirement to something much more reasonable. The leader should be sensitive to these overly bureaucratic requirements and ask periodically, "what reports are we requiring that tend to be falsified?"

Let me give an example to demonstrate my point. Years ago, a large agency of the federal government required that every day each sedan be given a 30-point inspection (which could take an hour or so to accomplish) by the first driver of the day. In most cases, the driver would sign off the report without inspecting anything. Under more enlightened leadership, the agency changed the inspection system. The new system requires that only one part of the vehicle be examined each day by the first driver of the day. If the car has not been driven for the last couple of days the driver may have to inspect three things. By the end of the month, everything will have been checked once—from battery cables to tire pressures to oil level to headlights. Drivers are perfectly willing to spend two or three minutes checking one or two systems. Integrity has returned to the reporting system and safety has not been compromised.

Leaders should evaluate the mission of the organization they are entrusted with in terms of its moral dimension. If the mission is ultimately based on individual worth, human equality, and human dignity, the leader cannot afford to ignore these values. For example, treating people unfairly or allowing unfair treatment to occur in the organization is inconsistent with the values that give that organization its fundamental worth.

Integrity is not something that can be put on and taken off as we go to and from work. People whose character is weak off the job do not have the character required to be top executives. For instance, an individual who cheats at golf, engages in spouse or child abuse, falsifies expense account records, or cheats on income tax forms, may also violate well established standards of institutional integrity at work. When such persons are placed in leadership positions, the final result is often failure in the short term or the long term; when they are at the top they will do serious damage to the organization or the institution that they lead.

Senior executives, much more so than junior leaders, need to be prepared to say "no" when ethics demand. Ethical decisions become even more complex as we grow in power, prestige, and rank. Good moral values will sometimes be in conflict. The leader must apply ethics with wisdom and maturity. This may be the greatest challenge and the greatest opportunity for the enlightened leader.

Unfortunately, many people feel that the values they developed in their youth are the ones that they will have for the rest of their lives. We all need to strive for moral ideals and, as we grow, to move the ideals to a higher level. People of character and integrity should seek to improve as they move to higher and higher positions of responsibility. Unfortunately, the opposite often occurs. As individuals climb up the slippery pole to success, they often sell their souls incrementally—making small compromises to their personal integrity to serve their ambitions or their egos. Junior executives who say to themselves, "I will never be like my big boss when I reach the top" all too often find themselves at the top, fifteen or twenty years later, acting very much like that big boss of the past who had such a low standard of ethics.

What is so often lost sight of by ambitious executives and subordinates is the functional nature of high integrity. Honesty *pays* in so many ways. It gives you and your employees high self-esteem; it helps to get attention and support if you honestly report on your problems; it enhances consistency in purpose and execution. On the other hand, falsification leads people in all kinds of unfortunate directions. If someone lies a lot or an organization engages in regular falsification of reports and records, it is awfully hard to remember what the truth is. In other words, lying, falsification of reports, and other forms of dissembling are not only ethically wrong but also dysfunctional. Make the case that the honesty is in everyone's best interest and you will raise the level of integrity in your organization.

In the early 1980s, a Chief of Staff of one of the military services received a briefing from his staff on the "Program" for the next five years. This Program outlined the staff's collective advice on how funds should be allocated yearly for the upcoming five-year period. When the briefing was completed, the Chief of Staff said quietly but firmly: "This is a dishonest Program; I will not submit it in its present form to the Secretary of Defense." The staff had developed the Program in a way that tried to maximize opportunities to get as much as possible of what that service needed. What was ignored or was, at least, circumvented, were some of the high priorities of the President and the Secretary of Defense. The staff was "gaming" the Program, and the Chief of Staff, being faithful to the letter and the spirit of the guidance he had received from the Secretary of Defense, was unwilling to sign the document.

Many issues of integrity in the highly politicized atmosphere of Washington are complex and fuzzy, but too often people take the manipulative road and integrity suffers. In the aftermath of the Iran-Contra affair and the parade of public officials indicted for their violation of the public trust, a wise observer of the Washington scene said that what the American people were looking for in their political leaders was *cleanliness*. Perhaps the great self-corrective nature of the American political system will move this system to better bipartisanship in foreign policy and to higher levels of integrity in our public servants—let's hope so. All leaders in government should remind themselves periodically of Grover Cleveland's candid comment, "Public office is a public trust."

The Wall Street scandals of the late 1980s demonstrate vividly the costs of low integrity to individuals (like Ivan Boesky), to their firms, and to the institutions they represent. Business ethics may not be as important as ethics in government, but it is not an inconsequential factor in the long-term health of Western capitalistic systems. George Washington perhaps said it best when he advised, "Labor to keep alive in your breast that little spark of celestial fire called conscience."

19

ORGANIZING PRIORITIES

the mission, the mission, the mission

The best leaders are passionate about the mission.

—*Reuben Harris*

The secret of success is constancy of purpose.

—*Disraeli*

There is a saying in real estate that there are three very important considerations when buying property: location, location, and location. The same can be said about leading a large organization in the sense that a leader must always remember the vital importance of the mission. If the leader is diverted into spending too much time on peripheral issues, the mission will suffer. The mission will also suffer if the leader does not encourage key subordinates to focus on the accomplishment of the organization's goals.

There seems to be an insidious tendency in large organizations for leaders' attention to be diverted by the unorganized and unprioritized demands of their schedule, their in-box, or their telephone calls. Only the most disciplined of leaders gain and maintain control of their schedules; and, even then, leaders must be able and willing to change as circumstances dictate.

Leaders must avoid wasting their time on unimportant issues. In addition, they should be particularly careful in not burdening subordinates at all levels with tasks that do not relate to the goals and priorities of the organization. This is a two-part problem. Some leaders get bored with a heavy commitment of time, energy, and emphasis on the organizational mission, and drift off into areas that may be fun and interesting but not directly related to the mission. These leaders often tie up key subordinates with projects and staff work that divert them from their most important responsibility, mission accomplishment. The second aspect of this dilemma is the followers and subordinate leaders who try to divert the attention of the leader away from the mission. Hence the relationship between leader and follower—as far as establishing goals and priorities and being faithful to them in the accomplishment of the organizational mission—is vital. Leaders and followers who reinforce each other in this regard contribute massively to the long-term health of any organization. Such phrases as "first things first" and "let's get back to basics" can be helpful in reinforcing this point.

Of course, a leader should not only speak and write about the importance of the mission; he or she must demonstrate personal involvement as well. If a leader is a president or dean of a college or university, that leader also should teach, not only to demonstrate a personal commitment to the goals of the institution, but to have direct interface with the students, staff, and faculty. Teaching is a good way to maintain an awareness of the bureaucratic and administrative problems that the faculty is facing relating to course preparation, syllabus development, printing plant capabilities, and problems that arise for teachers with publishers and guest speakers. If the leader runs a business, he or she should spend a good deal of time on the shop floor— even working on the production line, if feasible.

If some people must work on the night shift or the graveyard shift, the leader should also do so on occasion, if at all possible. Above all, a leader should conserve the "organizational energy" and do his or her very best to ensure that there is no organizational and individual time spent doing work with the sole purpose of making the leader look good, covering up mistakes, or otherwise detracting from the accomplishment of the mission.

One of the paramount requirements of leading large organizations is the need for the leader to joust constantly with the bureaucracy in order to ensure that the organization does not become complacent, stagnant, obsolete, or overly rigid in facing new challenges and opportunities. The problem of institutional rigidity is much greater than just the proclivity of large organizations to be conservative. With less than 20 percent of all professionals within large organizations being "innovators" it is not just organizational conservatism but also individual conservatism—especially in the middle levels of the bureaucracy—that can lead to policy rigidity. Many individuals tend to be more interested in survival, in staying out of trouble, in avoiding extra work, or in being promoted, than in carrying out the mission in as effective a way as possible.

Unfortunately, even strong innovators often hide their ideas in the bottom drawer of their desks until the organizational climate is just right for them to surface. This provides a challenge for a leader that is significant but not insurmountable. A climate of trust that helps the innovators come out of their shells can help create an atmosphere of excitement and creativity that can have a major impact on the future of the organization. General George C. Marshall and General Henry H. (Hap) Arnold, two of the great leaders of World War II, provided, throughout their long and distinguished careers, the climate for the creativity that led to some exciting and important results. Mission performance can be enhanced if innovation is encouraged.

George Marshall's commitment to planning, his knowledge of where the truly talented and innovative young professionals were, and his willingness to hire, nurture, and reward them, all played a vital role in the planning that was done just prior to World War II which led to the success of the Army and the Army Air Corps. Marshall's commitment to creativity played an important role in the establishment of a separate Air Force, the development of the Marshall Plan, and the significant long-range planning efforts in the War Department in the early 1940s, the State Department in the late 1940s, and the Department of Defense in the early 1950s. George Marshall provides a very useful model for an aspiring leader. As both a military and civilian government leader, he was absolutely superb—without peer in his time—in creating an atmosphere of high integrity, trust, creativity, and a sense of mission in all the organizations he led: the U.S. Army, the Department of State, and the Department of Defense. If you are looking for a model to pattern yourself after, George Marshall would be my recommendation.

Hap Arnold also had a strong commitment to planning and innovation. By the summer of 1943, he had created a post-war planning division that focused its full attention on the challenges and opportunities of the post-war world. He also created the RAND Corporation shortly after World War II. This was an important and innovative step. RAND soon became a model of a productive research agency where high-quality, policy-relevant, and, most importantly, interdisciplinary research could be accomplished. The creation of RAND and its impact on planning and policy making in the Air Force is historically unique. It set the pattern for many similar research groups which directly support governmental organizations or institutions.

Career patterns within most large civilian and governmental organizations may encourage dilettantism as individuals on the way to the top move rapidly from one job to the next. Within the last twenty years it has become a complimentary phrase in government, as well as in many business organizations, for someone to ask, "Can't you hold a job?" What this often means is that some individuals are so bright and successful that they are being moved onward and upward with great rapidity. However, when these individuals reach high-level leadership positions, they have become so accustomed to holding jobs for only one or two years that they often fail to dig deeply into organizational issues, problems, programs, and opportunities. As a result, they sometimes fail as leaders. Their time horizons have been habitually short, and any tendencies toward dilettantism are exacerbated by rapidly changing career patterns.

The transition from follower to big leader and from leader of a small organization to leader of a large one is, for many, a difficult one. Work patterns, peer relationships, time management, knowledge of details, generating candid feedback, and a myriad of other things change significantly when, at last, you get the chance to be a "big" boss. "Big" leaders must focus a considerable amount of their attention on the mission of the organization and not allow themselves to be diverted by the unprioritized demands of their telephone calls, their in-boxes, or their meeting and travel schedules. Subordinate leaders often have little choice but to follow a schedule that they have limited control over. Leaders of large organizations, if they choose to do so, can structure their own schedules to a considerable degree. Yet, too many leaders (who for years had little control) refuse to grab the bull by the horns and establish their *own* schedule and their *own* set of priorities.

The best of the big leaders do both, and, when they set their priorities, they place *mission* first. They also periodically check on how they are spending their time and their energies. They ask themselves periodically what their own "hidden agendas" are and how closely those agendas conform to the accomplishment of the mission. Since so much of mission accomplishment relates to the morale, effectiveness, and various agendas of key subordinates, the leader should spend a considerable amount of time nourishing leader-follower relationships.

When you are selected to lead a large organization, this new challenge should be approached with a very different mindset than is appropriate when you are selected for a normal staff or lower level leadership position. The mindset of a big leader should be different from the mindset of followers. Top leaders must have longer time horizons, must be willing to take risks to pursue important long-term goals, must be willing to empower subordinates with the authority to make and implement important decisions, and must be willing to give credit to subordinates for their ideas, energies, and sense of mission. Big leaders who don't develop this mindset may be good caretakers, gatekeepers, or managers, but are unlikely to be leaders who will make the kind of irreversible changes that will take their organizations in important new directions or lead to dramatically enhanced levels of mission accomplishment.

As a top leader of a large organization, you must realize that most of your subordinates want you to succeed, but a few will want you to fail. Most will carry out your guidance with enthusiasm and skill. Conversely, some will work against this guidance in hopes of undercutting your initiatives. In all large organizations, there will be individuals who tend to resist new initiatives unless they are their own ideas. The leader should, therefore, strive to capture the imagination and support of subordinates by letting them come up with new ideas. It is a wise leader, indeed, who listens carefully to subordinates and helps to turn their best ideas into organizational initiatives. Patience can pay off handsomely.

Great leaders exercise self-abnegation regularly and often; it is the sign of a great leader never to take personal credit for the success of the organization. Self-aggrandizement is a counterproductive quality in a leader. The leader who gets up in front of any group and states that the organization that he or she has led for the last two years was initially in terrible shape, but is in wonderful shape today, reveals a great deal. An objective observer would conclude that the organization was probably not as bad as this leader says it was two years ago, and not as good as proclaimed today. The truly mature leader will most likely say that the organization was in fine shape on arrival and any improvements that have taken place are the result of the talents and hard work of subordinates.

It is wise for a leader of a large organization to consider the point that Henry Kissinger made many years ago in his book *The Necessity for Choice*, "One of the paradoxes of an increasingly specialized, bureaucratized society is that the qualities required in the rise to eminence are less and less the qualities required once eminence is reached." Individuals who move into leadership jobs but who do not take a very hard look at themselves and who do not think about the differences between leading small organizations and large organizations, or between being a staff person and the leader, may be unable to provide the mature leadership required.

A question that a leader should often ask subordinates is, "How can I help you, and how can I make your job easier?" A related question is, "What am I doing that is making your job difficult and what is it about my style or my decisions that really bothers you?" If a leader doesn't ask these kinds of questions periodically, he or she is liable to become part of the problem rather than part of the solution. You may think you are doing a great job, while, in fact, other people may be spending a great deal of their time picking up after you or trying to reduce the impact of the mistakes that you are making.

A leader of a large organization should not only know what is happening within the organization and have solid operational and technical competence, but also should avoid spending a great deal of time in the details of the decision. Someone once suggested that one of our recent presidents didn't look at the forest and didn't look at the trees, but spent all his time looking at the leaves on the trees. This tendency toward micromanagement should be scrupulously avoided.

There is a fundamental paradox in leading large organizations that all leaders must understand and grapple with as best they can. The bigger the organization, the more trust is required, yet the harder it is to engender and reinforce trust. Leaders must not only trust subordinates, they must believe in their competence, perhaps more so than these subordinates believe in themselves.

A major problem in many organizations is a distorted notion of mission that some leaders and subordinates have. Some people will justify doing stupid, immoral or illegal things in order to "accomplish the mission." The mission of an organization cannot be separated from the values and principles upon which that organization is built. If a subordinate tries to justify using illegal or immoral means to accomplish a legal or moral mission, it is the role of the leader to remind that subordinate that there must be a close relationship between ends and means and both must be of high integrity. This may be one of the major enduring lessons of the Iran-Contra experience in the sixth year of the Reagan Administration.

A leader must be loyal to the boss, the mission, the people, the organization, the nation and, in some cases, to a supranational or international organization such as NATO, the Organization of American States, or the United Nations. Keeping these loyalties in proper perspective is a very important aspect of mature leadership. Almost everyone has a boss, and although leaders of large organizations have a great deal of autonomy, both in policy making and in geographic span, they still must answer to someone, whether it be their chief executive officers, a board of directors, the stockholders, the U.S. Congress, or the American people. Elbert Hubbard's remarks ring true on the issue of loyalty. He said, "Remember this. If you work for a man, in heaven's name, work for him. If he pays you wages which supply you bread and butter, work for him; speak well of him; stand by him and stand by the institution he represents. If put to a pinch, an ounce of loyalty is worth a pound of cleverness. If you must vilify, condemn and eternally disparage—resign your position, and when you are on the outside, damn to your heart's content, but as long as you are part of the institution do not condemn it."

Keeping an eye on the goals and making sure that priorities stay in order are not always easy tasks for a leader. For those in public service, the West Point motto is a useful guide: "Duty, Honor, Country." A public servant must be willing to resign if these fundamental principles cannot be upheld.

20

SCHEDULING YOUR TIME

disciplining yourself and your calendar

Time is the least thing we have of.

—Ernest Hemingway

Lost time is never found again.

—Benjamin Franklin

There has been much research in America on the issue of time management for executives. I have had the opportunity to survey that research. In addition, I have had a chance to observe at close hand how executives from other nations manage their time. Having worked directly for a German and for an Englishman in a large international headquarters in Northern Germany, I have gained some additional insights about how big leaders can best schedule and carry out their daily activities.

My British boss did not have either a daily or a weekly staff meeting. He interacted with the staff through staff papers or meetings and briefings on specific subjects. As an American, I was appalled by this approach, but soon learned that it worked in the international environment of a large staff. His leadership style also gave me great freedom to make decisions on his behalf, which I greatly appreciated.

My German boss was also uncomfortable with large staff meetings. He felt that they wasted a lot of time on the part of many people. He did agree with my plea for a weekly staff meeting, but only after I agreed to discipline the meeting in two ways. He wanted the meeting to last no more than an hour and he didn't want it to be a shortcut that would lead to sloppy staff work and quick but ill-considered decisions. My German boss met privately with me once or twice a week to philosophize about our mission and to share concepts and ideas on some of the better books on history and current issues that related to our mission. It was refreshing indeed to work for two men who did more than work on hot issues, who cared less about deadlines than they did about substance, and who had time to think deeply about long-term issues and opportunities.

President Eisenhower, who had had considerable experience in international staff environments, had a wonderful sense about where decisions should be made. He knew the difference between line and staff activities and had a good sense of the level at which decisions should be made. He disciplined his in-box by sending numerous decision papers back to the appropriate cabinet or agency head. To these papers he would attach short notes which indicated that he wanted the cabinet member to decide the issue. In time, he reduced the in-box material so that he had more time for the truly important or particularly sensitive issues, and for reflection and planning.

Don Rumsfeld, when he was Secretary of Defense, impressed all of us who worked in his outer office with the discipline of his schedule. Each week he would have a scheduling meeting where he would sit down with his key staff members to work out the next week's schedule. Attending the meeting were the Public Affairs man, the Congressional Relations man, Rumsfeld's executive assistant, and, in many cases, the Deputy Secretary of Defense. By developing a carefully thought out schedule that he stuck to quite carefully, Rumsfeld not only disciplined himself but also helped to discipline the entire process of decisionmaking. He scheduled some free time each day for contingencies and catch-up time. As a result of all this good planning and self-discipline, he almost always stayed on schedule and officials from throughout the Pentagon did not have to spend an inordinate amount of time cooling their heels in the outer office waiting for a meeting to start.

A CEO of a large research firm doing technical work for large companies and for the government uses a number of techniques to save precious time. For instance, he asks that meetings that he is not chairing start at 11:00 a.m. rather that 9:00 or 10:00 since he knows that many people have luncheon engagements and hence will move to the important issues quickly. He often times the length of his telephone calls and any subordinate who speaks to him for more that fifteen minutes on more than one or two occasions is later quietly counselled about being too long-winded. He sets a pattern of chairing short meetings (maximum time of one hour). He always announces the purpose of the meeting as it starts. If the purpose of the meeting is to reach a decision he will often say, "In about forty minutes I am going to ask for your views on a decision on the matter at hand." Also, those who do not speak up in a meeting are not normally invited back to the next meeting on the same subject. He feels that if, after a full hour of discussion, individuals who have nothing at all to say are probably wasting company time and money by attending the next meeting. Also this means that at the next meeting there will be a smaller group in attendance. There is a bonus with this approach: smaller groups are generally better at reaching decisions. Although there is a danger of establishing a climate for "group-think" with this approach, this CEO has found a way to avoid the problem: he always ensures that there is a strong "devil's advocate" present at all decision meetings.

There are many useful skills that an executive should develop as he or she moves up the ladder so that when the big job is taken the skills are well honed. A leader who knows how to dictate clearly to secretaries and to dictating machines can save precious time. Teddy Roosevelt was able to dictate as many as twenty-five letters an hour. (He would alternate back and forth between two secretaries.) He was able to complete most of a full day's work in a couple of hours through this dictation method. Fast and efficient dictation, of course, requires a secretary who can take dictation well and a leader who can organize thoughts effectively so that spoken words can be transformed into written words rather easily.

Another aspect of managing time is speed reading. Time can be better utilized if a leader can read very fast and pick up the essence of issues rapidly. A speed reading course, or just the practice of reading fast, is very helpful. If a leader can get through an in-box in an hour or two (whereas it might take a slower reader a full day), he or she will have more time available to be out with people, to have substantive meetings on important issues, and to be a true leader, rather than just a desk manager.

A third aspect of time management involves the maximum use of executive secretaries, administrative and special assistants, or deputies. Recruiting, testing, and hiring in this area is vitally important. A good executive secretary can help you manage your time well and watch your calendar carefully to make sure that the calendar reflects how you want to spend your day. Working very carefully with an executive secretary to work out a weekly or monthly schedule that fits your time clock, your body rhythms, and your priorities is an important aspect of time management.

Another one is maintaining "open time" every day. Open time should be for thinking, dealing with crises, seeing unexpected visitors, or dealing with fast-moving issues. If your calendar is filled from 7:30 a.m. until 6:00 p.m. at 15- or 30-minute intervals, you are poorly managing your time. You are probably getting into too much detail and not allowing yourself time to think. Subordinates who really need to see you on short notice may not reach you promptly.

As a general rule, a leader should not schedule more than one event an hour. A meeting with an individual, the corporate staff, one of your divisions, and other meetings should be scheduled in such a way that you will have time at the end of each before the next event takes place. In between these meetings, throughout the day, you should have time to return phone calls, work on items in your in-box, and to think and prepare for the next meeting. It is a reality of leading a large organization that there are increasing demands on your time. More and more people want and need to see you. Organizational priorities and your own priorities come into conflict. Leaders must work smarter, not harder. They must learn to say "no" to time wasters, and must deal with the "pathology of information" and information overload. The key is to understand that as the leader, you can manage your time—but it takes work, a disciplined outer office, a tough minded attitude, and planning.

21

TAKING CARE OF YOUR PEOPLE

mentoring, not cronyism

It is one of the most beautiful compensations of this life that no man can sincerely try to help another without helping himself.

—Ralph Waldo Emerson

Help those around you all you can. Every bit of help you give others will come back to you tenfold.

—E. B. Gallaher

A vital role for a leader is that of ensuring that subordinates are properly rewarded, promoted, and moved on to subsequent and more senior assignments in a deliberate and thoughtful way. A leader should identify the very best and help them get their next higher jobs within the organization. The leader should monitor their careers and help them achieve their full potential.

On the other hand, the leader should be very careful not to fall into the trap of cronyism. Pushing "his boys" (or "her girls") can often cause great morale problems within the organization. Practicing cronyism also can often hurt people by trying to help them; a leader who pushes a person into a big job before he or she is capable of handling that job, or who forces a protege on a subordinate leader, often does the protege a great disservice. In the second example, if the subordinate leader really does not want the individual, it is very likely that the individual's career, in the longer term, will be hurt by his or her working for that subordinate leader.

A related problem to dealing with cronyism is handling sycophancy. Unfortunately, in all large organizations there are individuals who are very skillful in pleasing the boss by bearing good news and by playing on the boss's ego. These individuals normally can be identified as those who are always looking for ways to make the boss happy, who worry about getting a lot of "face time" with the boss, and who are personally ambitious. There is a direct relationship between cronyism and sychophancy. Leaders must be sensitive to this significant problem area in large organizations.

A good rule of thumb for dealing with sycophants is to give them some counselling and then send them off to a job that takes them away from the corporate headquarters.

A leader also should pay particular attention to the "late bloomer." Within every organization, there are people of enormous talent who have matured later in life than their contemporaries. The late bloomer needs particular attention since personnel managers generally tend to overlook their career potential because this potential was not evident early.

A number of dysfunctional qualities sometimes develop in very talented people. The first dysfunctional quality is arrogance; no matter how talented an individual may be, if he or she becomes very arrogant, this person will be unlikely to succeed, over the long term, as a leader. Additionally, many individuals who exhibit potential early in their career do not live up to expectations. Leaders who are sponsoring individuals should periodically look at them with a critical eye to be sure that they are not pushing them beyond their capabilities. A general rule of thumb worth considering when you identify individuals with great talent and potential is the "one-push" rule. Give these individuals one strong upward push and then leave them alone. If the talent and potential are truly outstanding, those individuals will keep moving upward with no additional help from you. For those who have reached their ultimate level of potential and competence, further sponsorship to higher positions is a mistake. In a comprehensive analysis of why extremely competent young executives get "derailed" on the way to the top, the Center for Creative Leadership has shown that "overmentoring" often hurts these high achievers.

Many leaders make the mistake of confining their mentoring to those on the executive track. Mentorship also consists of identifying the best of the people at the lowest level and giving them a compliment and a boost. Leaders also must ensure that the organization is not "screwing over" the low-level subordinates—the people with the least power.

George Marshall probably provides the best model in the area of constructive mentoring. He had carefully identified people of great talent and potential during the first thirty-five years of his Army career. When he was selected by President Roosevelt to be the Chief of Staff of the Army in the late 1930s, he had a carefully compiled list of outstanding people in the Army and Army Air Corps. He used this list to select individuals for key staff and command positions in the immediate pre-war period. When war broke out, he used this list extensively to pick the top wartime leaders. To a very large extent, the U.S. military did extremely well in World War II because of General Marshall's careful sponsorship of people of talent, character, and leadership potential.

On the other hand, leaders should not bring a substantial number of former colleagues with them when they move to new positions. A leader who drags a large coterie of "the old gang" to the new job is likely to undermine the morale of the new organization. It also will be difficult to develop good rapport with new subordinates, and communication channels will be harder to establish. In addition, a leader will gain more credibility as a person of self-confidence and independent thought if that leader does not rely on a group of old (or not-so-old) cronies.

Finally, leaders of large organizations should provide guidance to subordinate leaders and personnel managers concerning the criteria for promotion. The promotion system must be fair and perceived to be so. Members of promotion panels or boards should be selected very carefully by the leader; the leader should give specific written guidance to each board. And the leader should meet privately with the head of the promotion board prior to the time that it meets. After the board completes its work, the head should report back to the leader and state specifically where the board was unable to fully carry out its guidance. Appendix A includes a useful checklist (Checklist 19) for promotion boards. It is a modified version of a checklist that was developed by the then Commandant of the United States Coast Guard, Admiral J.S. Gracey.

22

TEACHING
leadership essential

To teach is to learn twice.

—Joseph Jaubert

If you think education is expensive—try ignorance.

—Derek Bok

Good leaders tend to be good teachers and use various means to exercise "teachership" responsibility. Staff meetings, for instance, are marvelous teaching opportunities, as are welcoming briefings for new people in the organization, speaking engagements at professional schools, and, of course, teaching in one-on-one situations.

One useful technique is to make a videotape where the leader is introduced and then discusses the history of the organization, states the philosophy, goals, and priorities, and speaks about the importance of the mission and the important role of all the people. This tape has many uses. It can be shown to new employees, visitors, members of the media, etc. If resources permit, the videotape should be done professionally; it should be short (10 to 15 minutes), and it should be updated every year or two.

Part of teachership is planting good ideas in the minds of subordinates in such subtle ways that they soon feel these ideas are their own. A good leader probably has a lot of good ideas, but he or she will be a more effective leader if new ideas are perceived as and credited with having come from others within the organization. If those in an organization feel that it has reached high levels of excellence on its own without the direction of its leaders, when, in fact, many of the ideas that were implemented came from the leader, the leader has been very successful indeed. A leader should take silent satisfaction when such ideas are captured by others. It is a wise leader who takes the attitude of first grade teachers, who, at the end of the year, receive no thanks from the children, but know they have educated them well in their preparation for the next level. A good example is Fox Conner, who was the great teacher of Eisenhower, Marshall, and others. His teachership was quiet and subtle. He looked for no praise, but received great satisfaction from the brilliant performance of his students as they led the U.S. Army in World War II and in the post-war era.

A useful rule of thumb is the "2 percent idea" rule. No more than 2 percent of the ideas in an organization should emanate directly from the boss. If you are an "idea person" you should feed most of your ideas into the organization at a lower level and watch them bubble up to the top. If these ideas never reach you, they may not be as good as you thought they were!

A leader should not only be a teacher of subordinate leaders but should also teach them how to be teachers themselves, by establishing personal standards, by setting an example which others can emulate, by taking the time to teach, and by teaching systematically and regularly.

Periodic off-site retreats are excellent teaching opportunities. Leaders of organizations should invite their key subordinates to an area that is geographically removed from the normal work area for a two- or three-day retreat every year. The atmosphere should be a relaxed one. Attendees should remain on site overnight. Sports should be scheduled in the late afternoons (round robin tennis tournaments, volleyball, and softball work well as sports mixers). Spouses should not be included. Roommates should be paired so that each new individual rooms with a person who has been with the organization for some time.

The leader should open the retreat with a general statement of philosophy, goals, priorities, and concerns, and should review the past year by highlighting both the high and low points (a "fever" chart showing highs and lows can be helpful in this regard). The leader should emphasize the major upcoming events over the next few months and explain why they are important to the organization. The leader should thank subordinates for their outstanding work and encourage them to seek even higher levels of excellence next year. Initially, the leader also should establish the rules of the game for the retreat such as: all discussions are off the record and everyone should speak with total candor. The leader should ask questions, and questions on the part of subordinates should be encouraged: What successes have we enjoyed and what have been the secrets to these successes? What is really bothering you about the organization and my leadership style? What opportunities are we missing? What mistakes have we made or are we making? How can we make next year even more productive?

Before going on the retreat it is useful for the leader to send a short questionnaire to all the people who will be attending. The questionnaire should ask: What were the high and low points of the year? What new initiatives would you like to take next year? Who would be a good speaker from outside our organization for the retreat? What topics should we address at the retreat?

A major aspect of teachership is the maintenance of a reading program on the part of the leader. It is often said that the really tough jobs cause people to burn up intellectual capital because they stay so busy that they have little time to read, research, or reflect. Leaders who manage their time well can continue to read and gain insights from the best books and articles in their field.

Leaders should read good history, biographies, and autobiographies, as well as books on management, leadership, strategy, planning, and the long-term future. (See Appendix E for a short list of the better books on leadership.) One of the subjects that should be addressed on every off-site retreat is a list of the best books that the leader and his or her subordinates have read over the past year. Leaders should have cerebral energy and should demonstrate that energy not only by establishing a systematic reading program for themselves, but also by encouraging their subordinates to read important literature in their fields. Leaders should display books they have read lately in prominent places in their offices. As leaders read new books, these books should replace the ones that have been on the outer office coffee table in the previous weeks. In this way leaders can demonstrate visibly to all subordinates and visitors their commitment to a serious reading program. When they read a particularly outstanding book, they should buy a number of copies and give them to key subordinates. In addition, they should establish a system that allows the better professional journals to circulate throughout the organization.

One way for a leader to maximize the value of a reading program is to mark each book and to engage the author in a running conversation by making comments in the margin. Another technique is for the leader to mark the book with a "quote-file" notation that the executive secretary can then place in a file for the leader that can be used in speeches, articles, letters. In this way, leaders can ensure that future speeches have lots of fresh material that has been generated through the reading program. Through these techniques, leaders can keep up with their fields, with changing thoughts on leadership and management, and make future speeches at a high level of excellence and relevance.

When leaders go on trips, take vacations, or go home for weekends, they should try to avoid taking the in-box home. If leaders manage their time well, they should get to the bottom of the in-box by the end of the week and have time for outside reading on weekends, holidays, and trips.

A wonderful way to establish and maintain a productive reading program is to read, on a weekly basis, a significant number of book reviews. Most professional journals have book review sections. In addition, the *New York Times,* Sunday edition, has a first-rate book review section. A good general rule is: Don't buy a book until you have read at least two book reviews to ensure that reading the book is worth your valuable time.

Leaders who read a book each week are doing a reasonably good job of maintaining cerebral energy and intellectual curiosity. They should mix serious books of nonfiction that relate directly or indirectly to their chosen fields with "fun" books of fiction, biography, humor, travel, etc.

A useful technique to maximize the value of reading time is to read the first and last chapter of each book. If, after reading the first and last chapters, the leader has not been sufficiently inspired by the author's ideas and insights, reading the rest of the book may be largely a waste of time. In addition to reading on trips, weekends, and vacations, leaders should consider reading early in the morning, prior to going to work. Top executives who arrive at work late, by perhaps an hour or so, give their staff a chance to clean up the work of the previous day and to be ready for their queries and demands. A wonderful way to break the habit pattern of a lifetime of coming to work early is to schedule reading time at home prior to departing for work.

Since leaders should be visionaries and planners, they should spend some time reading books about the long-term future. There are a number of excellent mind-stretching books that can help leaders ask their planners the right questions. The following is a short list of books in this category: Kahn's *The Coming Boom*; Naisbitt's *Megatrends*; Cetron's *Encounters with the Future*; and Toffler's *The Third Wave*.

If a leader has been a good teacher, the organization will be in stronger shape, and the job for the next leader will be easier. If a leader is spending a great deal of time teaching, and only a modest amount of time problem solving, the leader probably has the priorities straight.

23

WORKING FOR THE BIG BOSS

the trials and opportunities of the subordinate

Wars may be fought with weapons, but they are won by men. It is the spirit of the men who follow and of the man who leads that gains the victory.

—*George S. Patton*

All bosses have a boss.

—*Anonymous*

Whenever I lecture on executive leadership, I almost always get the question: "I like many of your ideas and rules of thumb but how do I get *my* boss to follow the guidance?" My quick answer, which usually gets a laugh, is: "Have him or her read my book." The retort to this is usually, "Who is going to give it to him? Not *me!*" This gets to the heart of a very important question: What is the best way to get your boss to be a better and more enlightened executive without, at the same time, endangering your relationship with him or her, hurting your opportunities to contribute to the success of the organization, or endangering your career? Many executives feel that they have already demonstrated their ability to lead and hence don't read management or leadership books and certainly don't need advice on leadership from their subordinates. Many bosses would be insulted if one of their subordinates were to give them a book on leadership, for there would be an implied message that they needed help in this area.

So what are the answers for a subordinate who is working for a leader who has deficiencies in style, substance, or both? One approach is to live with the situation and take lots of notes on how *not* to lead, so that when the time comes for you to be an executive you will have a whole list of "not to's." The very worst boss I ever had was not very bright, was extraordinarily hardworking, and was the most ambitious individual I had ever known. He did not trust his subordinates even though the group was of high quality. Despite valiant efforts by over a hundred professionals, he was almost always in trouble with his superiors. Many times later, as I held some top executive position, I would be about to take action or make a decision when it would occur to me that my action would be something that this man might have done. I would pull up short and say to myself, "Oh no, that is *exactly* what *he* would have done. I'd better take another look."

In other words—some of the best lessons a subordinate can learn are what *not* to do and how *not* to do it. A really bad leader can teach you hundreds of things in this regard. In fact, you can learn a lot more from a bad leader than from a good leader, although the daily agony doesn't seem worthwhile at the time!

Another way to deal with weak or badly flawed bosses is to try subtly to assist them. By making an effort to help them you will gain the respect and affection of your colleagues, and you might even be able to make a difference. I have found that one of the best ways to help bosses is to corner them at a social gathering or at a sports event when they are relaxed and a bit more open to suggestions than they are when they're behind their desks. One approach that sometimes works is to start the conversation with something like "The folks on the line are really down in the dumps," or "I think we need to do something to improve the morale of our employees." If you use this kind of an opening, it is helpful to have some data that can demonstrate that there is, in fact, a morale problem of some kind. Such data might include unusually high absentee rates, an increase in the number of written complaints, negative feed-back from union leaders, or a higher-than-normal rejection rate off the production line. If the executive picks up on your point, you might be able to make suggestions which will improve both the situation and his or her credibility. Over time, you might be able to show him or her that some past decisions were faulty and need to be revisited.

I don't want to minimize the risks, however, and some bad bosses are not only reluctant to receive advice and criticism, but also are vindictive. (Executives who are reading this chapter might ask themselves, with as much objective introspection as they can muster, if they are receptive to criticism about their leadership.)

Another approach that may be effective is to suggest to the big boss that a subordinate executive be given an opportunity to attend a first-rate management or leadership program and to report back to the senior corporate officers on the insights that he or she gained from this experience. A better, but somewhat more risky approach, is to suggest that the leader himself or herself attend one of the week-long programs at the Center for Creative Leadership at Greensboro, North Carolina, the two-week course at the Kennedy School at Harvard University, or the five-week course at the University of North Carolina.

If you have to work for a weak boss it is sometimes useful to identify his or her specific weakness or weaknesses (as well as strengths) so you can help him or her build on the strengths and attack and improve on the weak areas. Furthermore, it may be helpful to think in terms of categories as far as bosses are concerned. Working for a wimp is different than working for a "Type A" boss, a power seeker, a laissez-faire individual, a mother hen, an ego tripper, or a hedonistic boss. Using commonly used phrases, let me describe some types of bosses and provide some hints on how to deal with them.

☐ **The Type A Boss** tends to micromanage, may be a workaholic, and may demand that subordinates work excessively long hours. He or she often overreacts to criticism, and is reluctant to delegate. Subordinates should try to reason with Type

A bosses about unrealistic deadlines, for instance, but if this doesn't work, standing up to them with firmness on a particularly unreasonable request will often get their attention and support: "I can get you an answer by the end of the day but it will be garbage that we won't be able to use. How about giving me a week and I'll come up with something that we can all be proud of (and the big boss will like)."

☐ **The Power Seekers** love to grab pieces of the action from parts of the organization which they do not control. "Turf" is terribly important to them and they almost never give anything up for fear that their power base may be diminished. Power seekers tend to love reorganizations, which they design themselves, that normally lead to more people, bigger budgets, and more centralization. Subordinates learn to treat power seekers with great care, but at times they can effect changes by demonstrating that delegation and empowerment will cause workers to work harder and more efficiently and therefore enhance the power seeker's prestige. Subordinates should explain with care that not only are the activities of the power seeker causing morale problems among the workforce, but that continuation of these activities may cause some of the more productive people to leave the firm or complain loudly to the power seeker's big boss. Leaders on "power trips" tend to be personally insecure and subordinates can sometimes play on these insecurities to help the power seeker curb his dysfunctional proclivities.

☐ **The Wimpy Boss** tends to be non-decisive and is afraid to take strong action in any direction. For instance, he or she would prefer to limp along with a weak subordinate than to fire that individual. His or her philosophy of leadership seems to be "no runs, no hits, and no errors." As a subordinate you can help wimpy bosses by making decisions for them and keeping them informed of the decisions that you have already made. If things go wrong, you, as the subordinate, will have to take the blame, and you may not get credit for the successes, but at least the organization will not be paralyzed. One technique that I have used with a non-decisive boss was to send him notes informing him about the action I was about to take and suggesting that if I did not hear from him within a week that I would press on. I indicated that I was willing to take full responsibility for my action in order to ease his mind. This is the "silence means consent" approach for subordinates.

☐ **The Laissez-Faire Boss** is usually a good one to work for in that he or she leaves you alone and allows you to make lots of decisions on your own. If your boss becomes too far removed from the action, you as a subordinate should try to keep him or her informed regarding important issues so that you don't stray too far from his or her views on these issues. You also have the opportunity to shape his or her views and the policy of the organization.

☐ **The Country Club Bosses** are so interested in their golf games, the next social event, or the next trip to the Bahamas that they get more and more out-of-touch with what is going on. Unlike a laissez-faire boss, who is interested but believes in delegation and empowerment, the country club boss has really lost interest and may not even be interested in helping you when you need assistance. Informal association with the boss at the next higher level or contact with key members of the Board of Directors if your boss is the Chief Executive Officer, may be useful if you need help or support from higher levels.

☐ **The Captured by the Staff Boss** normally has a large and talented staff that successfully steers the boss around. This can be quite satisfying for the staff, especially if the boss is willing to take decisions and to stick with them. However, this situation can be very frustrating to subordinate leaders in the plants, regional offices, and field activities, particularly when the leader makes poor decisions based on poor or biased staff advice. The leaders and managers who run facilities that are geographically removed from the corporate offices in the field can pursue issues through the staff in hopes of getting staff support for their ideas or initiatives. If this course is not successful, they can try to get the big boss to meet with them on a regular basis at a place where the staff is not present so they can lay out their concerns frankly and forthrightly with the boss. The direct approach can be helpful in certain circumstances: "We all admire you out here in the field but we are having a tough time with your staff." Or perhaps, "You have a great staff, but they have lost track with the real world out there."

☐ **The Boss with an Inflated Ego** only wants to hear that what he or she has done is right. This boss never wants to be challenged about his or her judgment, wisdom, or decisions. This boss becomes defensive when criticized and tends to contradict and threaten the subordinate who raises the criticism. If something good happens, the boss was the cause; if something bad happens, it is always someone else's fault. The subordinate should avoid direct criticism of this boss. By being very diplomatic, however, a subordinate can plant ideas into the boss's mind that the boss will soon think were his or her own. When the boss takes full credit for your idea or for the idea of one of your subordinates, do not challenge the point, but be sure to thank and reward the subordinate yourself.

☐ **The Mother Hen Boss** gives much too much specific guidance on even the most routine matters. This boss treats subordinates as if they were grammar school children or people of low intelligence. Subordinates should ask for a private session and diplomatically explain that they are fully capable of doing these routine tasks with little or no guidance. If this approach is not feasible, subordinates should find ways to keep so busy that they don't have time to meet with the boss for long guidance sessions. A third approach is to suggest to the boss that he or she handle certain issues so you can concentrate your efforts on other issues. Some mother hen bosses feel guilty if they are not busy all the time, and this third approach may help keep them from bothering you with too much guidance.

☐ **The Retired-in-Place Boss** is approaching the end of his or her career and no longer has much energy or interest in trying to do anything new or keeping in touch with subordinates and issues. The desire is strong on the part of many bosses to enjoy the fruits of their years of hard work by taking their last year or two off from any productive involvement in the leadership of the organization. Subordinates should try to see this as an opportunity to take initiatives on their own. As long as these initiatives require the boss to do little or no work, he or she may accept them. Another approach is to appeal to the boss in terms of establishing a legacy. Many bosses who are inclined to goof off will be motivated by a subtle appeal to their egos with the "we would like to see you retire on a high note" argument. Another useful approach is to try to get the boss to do a lot of travelling the last year. This should allow subordinates to take some initiatives while the boss is gone.

Too often, subordinates take a Pontius Pilate approach to poor leadership at the top. If the American economic, political, and military systems are going to thrive in the next century, it is incumbent upon subordinates and executives alike to take steps to improve the leadership of this nation's companies, government agencies, and nonprofit institutions.

Although this brief chapter was written largely for subordinates, there is considerable utility here for the executive. If you perceive that subordinates are doing some of the things suggested above, it may well be that *you* are the source of many of the problems your organization is experiencing. Few leaders are as good as they think they are, and listening for signals is an important part of the leadership equation.

Followership and leadership are closely linked. Leaders need good followers and followers need good leaders—and both groups need the positive interaction and chemistry between the two groups if the institution, organization, or company is to thrive. Followers should remember that no executive wants to fail, that few leaders want to be labelled a wimp, a geek, or an autocrat by their subordinates. Followers who understand that leadership brings out the very best or the very worst in an individual and who are willing to help the leader reach for the best can be marvelous contributors to excellence and good morale.

Followers can learn a great deal by observing leaders, both good and bad. By seeking and obtaining as many opportunities to exercise leadership as the delegation, empowerment or apathy of the boss will allow, followers can prepare themselves for the great challenges and opportunities that lie ahead. Followers can grow considerably if they do more than simply accomplish what their job description requires. A regular reading program, periodic attendance at executive development seminars, and the keeping of a file of good quotations, humorous stories, and jokes can help. In addition, would-be leaders should actively seek out leadership opportunities in the local community, in church or temple, and in professional associations and clubs.

As you work your way up the corporate or institutional hierarchy, try to keep in mind that, when you become a leader, large numbers of people will be relying on you to be the very best that you can be.

24

WRAPPING UP
putting it all together

American organizations have been over managed and under led.
—Warren Bennis

The greatest problem facing America may be the short supply of
'gifted generalists.'
—Harlan Cleveland

This book has been designed to give a leader practical thoughts
on how to run large organizations. Although the Appendices
provide a number of checklists, it is important to emphasize
that complete reliance on "checklist" or "cookbook" leadership can be a mistake. Anyone who runs an organization but
cannot adapt to the situations not contained in checklists in
conducting day-to-day activities is doomed to fail as an enlightened leader. Therefore, readers should accept the ideas, insights, and checklists that are provided with a certain amount
of skepticism. Much that happens in big organizations is truly
unique; however, the lessons of others may be helpful as a
leader struggles with current problems.

It is important for leaders to do their own thinking, to read
widely, and to talk with and listen to others within and without
their own organizations. Leaders should never rely on one key
associate or assistant to do their thinking for them. If they do
so, in a very real sense they are no longer leaders.

"Before a leader makes a decision, it is useful to ask a few
questions. Who is going to be mad? How mad? Who is going to
be happy? How happy?" This insight from Paul Appleby is use-

ful, for it highlights the need for a leader to anticipate the reactions of subordinates and others who may be affected by key decisions. Anticipating reactions should not paralyze a leader preparing to make decisions, but considering reactions will help you to frame the right questions before you make those leadership decisions.

Leadership is not synonymous with authority. It is, to a very considerable extent, a value which is entrusted to the superior by the subordinate. It embodies an emotional, often spiritual, investment by the subordinate in his superior, a gift of trust. To a great extent, the subordinate defines the conditions under which trust is given. He prescribes those qualities, characteristics, and values his superior must possess in order to be accepted as his leader. It is the wise leader, indeed, who understands and nurtures the relationship between superior and subordinate.

Admiral James Stockdale, who has written powerfully and meaningfully about leadership, has good advice for all of us. He believes that individuals who are not willing to discipline people, who are unwilling to remove people, and who crave to be loved, all tend to be poor leaders. Stockdale states, "Truly, leaders must be willing to stake out territory and declare enemies." As we train and educate leaders, it is more important to teach key people how to deal with failure than how to deal with success.

It is vitally important that leaders do not let the urgent force out the important in their day-to-day activities. They should spend their talents lavishly rather than hoarding them. Leadership should be a giving rather than a taking experience. The attitude of the leader is important because the posture assumed in day-to-day activities can have a great impact on the morale of an organization. If the leader is a negative person, it is likely that subordinates will adopt a negative disposition. On the other hand, if the leader is cheerful, the cheerfulness will spread throughout the organization. People want to feel good about themselves, their organization, and what they are doing.

Many leaders fail to fully exploit the various means available to motivate their people to higher levels of commitment, performance excellence, and integrity. All leaders, for instance, should take a hard look periodically (at least annually) at their various formal and informal incentive programs. Is the annual bonus system robust enough and fair? Is it perceived as being fair by employees at all levels? How effective are various Employee of the Month, Manager of the Year, Salesperson of the Quarter programs? Are the right people being selected and is the award being properly publicized? Does the recipient get a monetary award, time off, or a certificate? Are these awards the ones that your employees really want, or are there others that would have more impact?

Don't forget to develop awards that reward the average worker for above-average work. The "most improved" kinds of awards are very useful motivators to the lower level folks who otherwise might never be singled out for recognition.

Many suggestion and "new ideas" programs focus on only one part of the enterprise and neglect other areas. Awards for the design of the better wrench to improve assembly line or maintenance efficiency are fine and should be continued. However, the person who comes up with the next new concept or strategy for manufacturing may impact on the bottom line much more significantly. He or she should not only be rewarded for the great new concept; he or she should also be motivated to continue to think about conceptual innovation.

There is lots of empirical evidence showing that positive expectations lead to positive results. This "Pygmalion effect" should serve as a beacon of truth and inspiration for all leaders—tell people that they are outstanding and that they can accomplish a great deal, and in most cases they will meet or exceed your expectations.

Jack Jacobs has pointed out that "A leader of a large organization may often have to accept rotten circumstances in order to make overall progress. The high-level leader who will accept nothing less than the perfection that can be achieved at great cost will lose everything. This is not to say that standards must be low; on the contrary, it is at the highest levels that high standards originate. But the leader has to have the kind of long-range vision that will overlook short-term setbacks." The leader must understand a truism of large organizations: "The perfect can be the enemy of the good." A leader crosses an important milestone when signing that first imperfect, but wholly adequate, staff paper without editing or changing it personally.

Leadership functions must be shared with "lieutenants." The organization will become healthier as the leader creates more centers of leadership within the organization. Leaders must take particular care in nurturing their relationships with their deputies. The deputy leader must be given authority to make decisions in the absence of the leader and those decisions must be supported enthusiastically by the leader. The deputy should be included in all substantive meetings, discussions, and decisions so that the entire institution understands that the deputy has authority, responsibility, and credibility.

If the leader comes from a specialized area, whether it be marketing, personnel, logistics, engineering, operations, or any other, there must be personal initiative for the leader to grow beyond that specialized field. A true leader will always be fundamentally challenged rather than repelled by complexity. Leaders should focus primarily on opportunities, not on problems.

Leaders must be generalists; those who select individuals for leadership positions should pick individuals who have the capacity to grow and to become gifted generalists. If the leader is to ensure organizational creativity and innovation, there must be tolerance for the creative fanatic who, in many cases, is the force behind important innovations. The leader must realize that large and complex organizations often suppress new ideas, new opinions, and new alternatives. Leaders must fight against the bureaucratic tendencies to create watered-down compromises that are often less-than-desirable solutions. There is a sign on a rural road in upstate New York that says, "Choose your rut carefully; you will be in it for the next 25 miles." A leader is someone who identifies the "ruts" within an organization and makes sure that individuals or groups of individuals do not stay in these "ruts" for the next twenty-five weeks, twenty-five months, or twenty-five years.

In every organization, there are many people who are not

pulling their share of the load because of their own incompetency, laziness, poor attitudes, psychological difficulties, bad habits, or family problems. It is the role of the leader to deal with these people and to motivate them, counsel them, isolate them, or, as a last resort, remove them. One of the frustrating things about dealing with large organizations is the difficulty in removing incompetent individuals. A leader must be very aggressive in this regard; although it might take a great amount of time and effort to deal with incompetents, the effectiveness and morale of the organization depend upon maintaining high standards of competence and integrity. A leader must be willing to establish, maintain, and enforce those standards.

I have purposefully not written a chapter on women or on racial or ethnic minorities in leadership positions because it is my strong belief that the art of leadership is not something that is unique to any one group of people. However, I do feel that there are different cultural and historical environments that impact significantly on the rules of the game for leadership in various parts of the world. For instance, leading citizens in the Soviet Union is very different from leading citizens in the United States. I also feel that leadership requirements vary considerably in different historical settings. For instance, leadership in the historical context of the Napoleonic era in France was different than it is today in a France, which now enjoys a rich tradition of democracy that has extended over more than a century.

Within the democratic tradition of Western nations, the ground rules are quite similar whether the organization is being led by a woman, a Hispanic, a black, an Asian, or another member of a minority group. Dynamic and effective female leaders such as Margaret Thatcher from Great Britain, Indira Gandhi from India, and Jeane Kirkpatrick from the United States, have shown that women do superbly in leadership positions and generally follow the ground rules for the cultural environment in which they operate. The same can be said for blacks, Hispanics, and other minority groups in America.

Those who would make a big differentiation between men and women (or between or among racial groups) in leadership roles tend to do so based on a few personal experiences rather than upon an examination of the large amount of empirical data that is now available. Readers who are interested in the topic of women in leadership positions may like to read *Breaking the Glass Ceiling: Can Women Make it to the Top in America's Largest Corporations?* (Addison-Wesley, 1987.)

The real question is not whether women or people from minority groups can be great leaders or not: it has already been proven that they can; the question is how they can get the jobs that will lead to the big leadership posts.

People who are only as smart as their in-boxes, their immediate staff, their personal experiences, and their television sets, are not smart enough or wise enough to lead large organizations well. Great leaders have become great by hard work, by cultivating an inquiring and open mind, by reaching out widely to people for ideas and insights, and by reading broadly and critically.

There is no activity in human endeavor that is more fascinating, more challenging, and more rewarding than leading organizations with an important mission. The leaders who are willing to grow, learn, listen, acknowledge mistakes, teach subordinates, set goals, and maintain high standards are leaders who can help lift an organization to new heights. Tom Cronin challenges each of us when he writes: "Leaders have those indispensable qualities of contagious self-confidence, unwarranted optimism and incurable idealism that allow them to attract and mobilize others to undertake tasks these people dreamed they could not undertake." This is the true task of the leader.

APPENDIX A
checklists for busy leaders

Whatever advice you give, be short.

—Horace

The following checklists are provided to help leaders accomplish several of the important tasks that confront them. Operational checklists can be important in two major areas: in ensuring a task that must be done very quickly is accomplished in proper order, and in ensuring that a vital step or element is not left out. Leadership checklists serve the same basic purposes.

These checklists are not substitutes for judgment, but they can trigger the thinking process and make the task at hand somewhat easier.

1. Transition Checklist
2. Communications Checklist
3. Hiring Checklist
4. Performance Counselling Checklist
5. Firing Checklist
6. Hang-Up Checklist
7. Thank-You Checklist
8. "Antenna" Checklist
9. Cynical Expressions to Listen For Checklist
10. Phrases to Avoid Checklist
11. Decisionmaking Checklist
12. Executive Skills Checklist
13. Introspection Checklist
14. Press Conference and Media Interview Checklist

---

1. Transition Checklist

The following are useful questions to ask when you have been selected to assume a leadership position. They are also useful questions to answer for the incoming leader if you are stepping down.

☐ What is the mission?

☐ What are the organization's
—goals?
—priorities?
—plans?
—programs?
—budgets?

☐ What is the size and structure of the organization?

☐ What means of communications will I have?
—newspaper/newsletter?
—radio?
—television?
—staff meetings?
—formal and informal seminars?
—social gatherings?

☐ Who reports directly to me?
—how many?
—why?
—why not others?

☐ Who is my boss?
—what is his or her leadership/management style?
—what is his or her means of communication to me?
—what does he or she expect of me and when?

☐ Am I responsible for geographically separated units?
—do they report directly to me?
—do they report indirectly to me?

☐ Which organizations, corporate staff offices, and individuals should I visit?

—in what order?
—how often (for subsequent visits)?

☐ What is the standard of integrity?
　　—have there been recent violations of these standards?
　　—how frequent and what was the outcome?

☐ What are the standards of performance?
　　—how are they measured?
　　—what are the results of recent
　　　—outside inspections?
　　　—self-inspections?
　　　—audits?

☐ What documents should I read?
　　—in what order?
　　—is there an annual organizational history? if not, why not?
　　—is there a book of standard operating procedures; organizational regulations?
　　—what are the most important plans?
　　—is there a long-range plan? if not, why not?

☐ What skeletons are in what closet?
　　—organizational skeletons?
　　—personal skeletons?

☐ Where are the personnel strengths, shortages, and weaknesses?

☐ What is the condition of the industrial plant, buildings, unit equipment, etc.?

☐ What are the major logistics problems?

☐ What are the toughest problems and issues I should expect to face during the first few months?

☐ How often do the top leaders and their immediate subordinates go to "off-site" seminars together?

☐ Did the previous leader have a philosophy letter?
　　—what should I include in my philosophy letter?

2.   Communications Checklist

Many leaders fail to use fully the means of communications that are, or can be, made available to them. This checklist may be helpful to ensure that opportunities are not missed.

☐ Is there an organization newspaper?
    —how often is it published?
    —what is its quality?
    —does the leader have a space reserved for a weekly/ monthly column?
    —how wide is the readership?
    —what percentage of the readership actually reads the leader's column?
    —is there a feedback channel?
        —letters to the editor?
        —action line?

☐ Does the leader have regular access to:
    —radio?
    —television?
    —closed-circuit television?

☐ Are there regular staff meetings?
    — minutes taken, published, and circulated?
    —do participants feel free to raise issues?

☐ Are there work unit meetings?

☐ Is there a public affairs office?
    —does the public affairs director report directly to you? if not, why not?
    —what are the public affairs director's ideas on how best to communicate to the people?

☐ Are subordinate organizations being publicly praised and thanked? In what ways and through what means?

☐ Is there a movie or videotape that explains the organization to new people, visitors, guests, families, community leaders, etc.? If not, why not?

☐ Do I take advantage of the informal means of communication, taking coffee breaks with subordinates, participating in bowling leagues or golf tournaments, and attending company social and sporting events?

3. Hiring Checklist

When the organization is hiring a subordinate for a key position, a personal interview is recommended in order for the leader to get a "feel" for the individual and for the "chemistry" between the leader and the prospective subordinate. If a face-to-face interview is not possible, an interview by telephone can be an acceptable substitute. These questions are valuable ones to ask during interviews. When you "check the individual out" with other individuals, some of these questions can also be useful.

- ☐ Do you want the job? Why?
- ☐ What talents, qualities, and strengths would you bring to this job?
- ☐ What are your weaknesses?
- ☐ How long would you like to hold this job?
- ☐ What is your leadership/management style?
- ☐ If I asked a subordinate of yours to describe you and your leadership style, what would be the response?
- ☐ If you are not selected, whom would you recommend for this job?
- ☐ What are the best books you have read in the last few years? What insights did they provide you?
- ☐ What are your long-term personal goals?
- ☐ Do you expect to be promoted soon?
- ☐ Are there any "skeletons in any closets"?
- ☐ Whom in your present organization do you admire the most and why?
- ☐ What is the standard of integrity in your present organization?
- ☐ Are you considering any other positions?

☐ If I select you for this job, would you take it as your first choice over other positions you are considering?

☐ How many people have you led or supervised in your career?

☐ Have you ever fired anyone? Have you ever been fired?

☐ What experience do you have with
  —operations?
  —planning?
  —finance/marketing?
  —research and development?
  —personnel?
  —computer systems?

☐ Have you had any setbacks in your career?
  —if so, what were the most significant lessons learned from the setbacks?
  —what organizational setbacks have you observed at first hand?

☐ What is the toughest problem you have ever faced in your professional career? How have you handled it?

☐ What questions have I failed to ask you?

☐ What questions do you have for me?

4. Performance Counselling Checklist

This checklist can be a helpful guide when you have one-on-one sessions with your subordinates. Any checklist used in this regard should be committed to memory so that the one-on-one session does not become too formal or structured. Prior to your semiannual series of one-on-one sessions, you may wish to circulate a list of questions along the general lines of this checklist to give your subordinates an idea of the questions you are going to ask and the points you are going to cover. This will help the subordinate be better prepared and more at ease.

- ☐ What aspects of this organization do you like the most?

- ☐ What areas around here bother you the most?

- ☐ What are your ideas for improving this organization?

- ☐ What organizations, factories, programs, staff functions, branch or regional offices, etc., should we divest ourselves of, and on what kind of schedule (now, next year, five years from now, etc.)?

- ☐ In your judgment, who are the most innovative, helpful, and cooperative people in this organization?

- ☐ What are your personal goals while you are in this organization?

- ☐ Where and to what job would you like to go next? Why and when?

- ☐ What do you consider to be your most significant weaknesses?

- ☐ What self-improvement programs do you have underway?

- ☐ What do you think your chances are for promotion to the next rank or position, and in what time frame?

- ☐ What bothers you the most about my decisions and my leadership style?

☐ What three things cause you to waste your time the most?

☐ Is there anything I am doing that wastes your time?

☐ What kind of personnel development program does your
    department have for minority groups? How successful is
    it?

☐ What are the goals you have established for your organi-
    zation?

☐ Please evaluate the performance of the organization,
    unit, or group that you led over the past year (or in the
    period since we last had a one-on-one session). Please
    outline the high and low points of the period.

---

5. Firing Checklist

This difficult duty can become somewhat easier if it is accomplished systematically and if the leader can maintain a sense of concern and empathy while, at the same time, sticking with the decision to remove the individual. During the one-on-one session, the individual should be given adequate time to vent displeasure or disagreement with the decision. The leader can gain useful insights about problems within the organization from passive listening during this session.

☐ Outline reasons for the decision:
   —loss of confidence in subordinate's abilities.
   —incompetence:
      —as a supervisor/leader/manager.
      —as a writer.
      —as a teacher.
   —lack of ability to meet deadlines.
   —lack of integrity.
   —poor attitude.
   —chronic absenteeism.
   —inability to get along with boss/peers/subordinates.
   —inablity to keep up with rapidly changing technology.

☐ Ask what he or she might want to do next and how you could help.

☐ Ask what lessons can be drawn from this setback.

☐ Ask if there are any things about the organization that you should know.

☐ Offer professional assistance (psychiatrist, financial advisor, lawyer) if appropriate.

☐ Explain what kind of effectiveness report to expect and to what extent, if any, you would be willing to give references to future prospective employers.

6.   Hang-Up Checklist

All leaders should know their "hang-ups" and articulate them to their subordinates when they assume their leadership position and periodically thereafter. Since a hang-up checklist is very much a personal statement of the leader's biases, concerns, idiosyncrasies, etc., each leader must prepare his or her own. The following is a proposed hang-up checklist. It is illustrative only and should be used as a very general guide.

- ☐ Low levels of integrity.
- ☐ Careerism/hyperambition.
- ☐ Lack of style.
- ☐ Missing deadlines.
- ☐ Being used.
- ☐ Rumormongering.
- ☐ Parochialism.
- ☐ Retirement on the job.
- ☐ Dilettantism.
- ☐ Not telling the full story.
- ☐ Authoritarianism.

7. Thank You Checklist

These are a few ways to thank the people who do so much to make you organization thrive.

Many thanks for:

☐ your contribution to the mission.

☐ your integrity.

☐ making my job easy.

☐ adding elegance and style to our organization.

☐ caring.

☐ your commitment to excellence.

☐ your marvelous attitude.

☐ your willingness to take on the tough jobs.

☐ your willingness to work cooperatively with people.

☐ your willingness to tell it like it is.

☐ your willingness to take risks.

☐ your courage.

☐ your self-sacrifice.

☐ your creativity.

☐ your courtesy.

☐ your sincerity.

☐ your love.

☐ your sensitivity.

☐ setting and maintaining high standards.

☐ meeting our goals.

☐ exceeding our goals.

☐ your ideas.

- ☐ your vision.
- ☐ your tolerance.
- ☐ your leadership.
- ☐ your teachership.
- ☐ your contributions.
- ☐ your dedication.
- ☐ your professionalism.
- ☐ your receptivity to ideas.
- ☐ your sound advice.
- ☐ your common sense.
- ☐ your responsiveness.
- ☐ your loyalty.
- ☐ your honesty.
- ☐ your willingness to criticize constructively.
- ☐ your ability to rise above parochialism.
- ☐ your cerebral energy.
- ☐ your ability to conceptualize.
- ☐ your style.
- ☐ your maturity.
- ☐ your lack of pettiness.
- ☐ your magnanimity.

---

8. "Antenna" Checklist

It is important for all leaders to stay "tuned in" to patterns of activities of their organizations, to be open to feedback and to criticism, and to listen to their subordinate leaders. This checklist can be helpful to leaders who wish to stay in touch over the entire period of their leadership.

- ☐ Unethical phrases to listen for:
    - —pencil whipping.
    - —fudging the figures.
    - —cooking the numbers.
    - —gaming the program.
    - —bending the facts.
    - —manipulating the data.

- ☐ Careerist phrases to listen for:
    - —"I don't trust the personnel system."
    - —"Who is your sponsor?"
    - —"I don't have a sponsor."
    - —"You need to get on board."
    - —"I need to get my ticket punched."
    - —"It's not what you know, it's who you know."
    - —"I need some face time with the boss."
    - —"I want a high visibility job."
    - —"Joe 'talks a good game.' "
    - —"To get ahead you have got to go along."
    - —"You need to quit 'fighting the problem.' "
    - —"Be careful—the boss likes to 'shoot the messenger.' "

- ☐ Signals indicating the Peter (or Paul) Principle (see page 98) is at work:
    - —"It sure takes X a long time to get something done."
    - —"Why can't X seem to focus on the issue?"
    - —"I can never get Z to take a position on anything."
    - —"Have you noticed that X is always defensive?"
    - —"Y has no initiative."
    - —"Z has lost his (or her) drive."

—"X was a great staff member, but seems lost as a leader."

—"Y's folks are afraid of him (or her)."

—"Z's people are frustrated."

—"X has a bad case of 'not invented here'—is never open to ideas from the outside."

—"Y seems to complain all the time."

—"Z is on the road a lot—I wonder who is minding the store?"

—"X never seems to make any deadlines."

—"Is that job too big for Y?"

—"Z is out of touch."

—"How come X surrounds himself (or herself) with cronies?"

—"Y has no sense of outrage."

—"Z lets the system screw over his (or her) people."

9.   Cynical Expressions to Listen For Checklist

Executives who listen carefully as they wander around can pick up cynical expressions that may tell a lot about their leadership styles and the organizational climate.

☐ *"When is the ten o'clock meeting going to begin?"*
The message here is that you are poor time manager and have a bad reputation of being behind schedule. Your subordinates may feel not only that you are wasting their time as they cool their heels in the outer office but also that you have no interest in the fact that they also have a schedule to meet and subordinates waiting to meet with them.

☐ *"I wonder how those folks in the other departments avoid Saturday work call?"*
You may be a workaholic who is guilty of drawing in a lot of people for weekend work that may not be necessary.

☐ *"When is the boss going on his next trip?"*
There could be a number of different signals here. Your subordinates may be suggesting that they want you out of town so they can get something worthwhile done. Or they may want you out of town so they can get a day or two with their families. Or they may be wondering why you are doing so much travelling and so little work.

☐ *"It is tough to fire anyone around here."*
You may be guilty of protecting employees so much that you are tolerating a number of incompetents at lower levels in your organization. It may also mean that you have not supported your subordinate leaders when they have tried to fire somebody.

☐ *"It sure is hard to get on the boss's schedule."*
Perhaps you are so over-scheduled that your subordinates can't figure out a way to get in to see you on important issues.

☐ *"Does the boss ever sleep?"*
Another signal that your workaholic proclivities may be hurting morale.

☐ *"One thing we do around here well is waste time."*
Are you doing things and taking actions that waste the time of your people?

☐ *"It sure is tough to get a decision around here."*
Leaders often don't realize how indecisive they are. This comment may help them get the picture.

☐ *"Does the boss ever go home?"*
You may have established a pattern of workaholism and micromanagement.

☐ *"Who was the last guy the boss talked to?"*
This may be a symbol that you have a tendency to be swayed by the latest input.

☐ *"I wish I knew what the policy was around here."*
You may not have established or articulated your policies very well.

☐ *"I sure wish I knew how I stood around here."*
You may be failing to counsel, compliment, or both.

☐ *"The rats are deserting the sinking ship."*
This may signal that your employees are reading the departure of some people as a sign that the organization is going downhill fast.

☐ *"I wonder when that 'always-open door' ever opens."*
You said your door was always open but you didn't really mean it.

---

10.   Phrases to Avoid Checklist

Leaders often use phrases that are counterproductive in large organizations. Although some of these phrases work and work well in small organizations, leaders should ask themselves if they are sending the right message in the environment of a large organization. From my experience, here are a few commonly used phrases that just don't work well for the top executives of a large organization.

☐ *"Make it happen now."*
This statement by a leader often leads to someone on the staff cutting corners to the point of violating personal or organizational integrity. It possibly leads to decisions that are not well coordinated, thoughtful, or in accordance with established priorities.

☐ *"I don't get mad—I get even."*
This is an intimidating statement that lacks dignity and creates a climate of fear throughout an organization.

☐ *"I don't like surprises."*
This commonly used phrase seems reasonably benign, and useful, but it often leads to many decisions being pushed up too high—an impediment to innovation and initiative on the part of subordinates.

☐ *"My door is always open."*
This phrase is often a useful one in small organizations, but when used by a leader of a large organization, it is frequently misleading. The leader of a large organization who always keeps his or her door open to subordinates at all levels often becomes buried in minutiae. Leaders who say their doors are always open when this is not in fact the case will soon find they have created an atmosphere of cynicism and skepticism about their availability to subordinates.

☐ *"Be sure to keep me informed."*
This is a sure-fire way to ensure an overly full in-box and

lots of phone calls, both day and night. The phrase is the antithesis of delegation and empowerment of subordinates—two key principles in leading large and complex organizations.

☐ *"Just give me the bottom line."*
Bosses who use this phrase often begin to lose touch with the essential elements of important issues. A better phrase is "I need the bottom line, but I also need to understand how you got there."

☐ *"We can't handle any new initiatives this year."*
This kind of guidance is counterproductive to taking an organization to higher levels of good planning, competence, and efficiency. The leader who cuts off new initiatives because of budgetary or other reasons may be making a major mistake. If he or she is actively engaged in divestiture activities to unload organizations or missions that are no longer needed, he or she ought to be able to develop, encourage, and implement new initiatives every year.

☐ *"If it ain't broke, don't fix it."*
This commonly used phrase seems to make a great deal of sense, but, in fact, is often an impediment to progress in an organization and an invitation to mediocrity. Just because an organization is running well does not mean that innovation, new ideas, and new initiatives aren't helpful. If "it" is not broken, you should not fix it, but, on the other hand, if "it" is not broken, it still might be improved incrementally with initiative and new ideas.

☐ *"My mind is closed on that issue."*
This is an unwise phrase on two counts: First, a leader's mind should never be totally closed on any issue since changing circumstances or new data may require a readdressal of issues. Second, the phrase sends a signal of great rigidity. Leaders should remind themselves to avoid being like the colonel in *The Bridge on the River*

Kwai—it was right to build the bridge, but, later, it was just as right to destroy it.

☐ *"I'll call in every morning to get an update."*
The leader who can't go on a trip or on a holiday without checking in with his or her office every day is making a very important statement about his or her approach to leadership. If something is really important and you have trained your front office people well, you will certainly get a call. Why not let your deputy run the show for a few days? It may do you, your company, and your deputy, a lot of good. This is called leadership development. It is also called trust.

☐ *"Let's agonize over this issue."*
This phrase, which is used on occasion in the U.S. Government setting, is disliked by subordinates for obvious reasons. A better phrase would be "let's debate this issue" or "let's build a decision matrix on this issue." Decisionmaking should be a challenging experience; it should not normally be an agonizing one.

☐ *"I don't care how you get it done, just do it."*
This is an invitation to your subordinates to take shortcuts, be dishonest, or act illegally. Many leaders learn the hard way that this can be an invitation to disaster.

☐ *"There is no way a woman [black, Hispanic, bachelor, etc.] will get that job."*
Discrimination on the part of the top executive has a very serious impact on an organization. Sexual, racial, cultural, ethnic, or any other discrimination on the part of the leader is immediately transmitted throughout the organization. Even a small amount of subtle discrimination at the top can lead to major discrimination and morale problems at lower levels.

☐ *This organization was in bad shape until eighteen [or twelve, or whatever] months ago."*
If it was eighteen months ago that you took charge, you have just revealed a great deal about yourself, your abil-

ity to be introspective, and your objectivity. The message that you are conveying is that the previous boss must have been a lousy leader, that the staff and subordinate leaders aren't capable of excellent performance unless they are blessed with you as their boss, and that if you should leave for another job, retire, or die, the place will probably fall apart. A more magnaminous (and probably more accurate) way to discuss the subject would be to say, "The last boss was super and the plans he put together were first-rate. I am pleased that I have the kind of team that can carry out these plans and take the organization to even higher levels of excellence."

11. Decisionmaking Checklist

Top leaders should make the decisions on the big issues and the sensitive issues. Before finalizing each decision, the leader can use this checklist to help improve the quality of the decision and avoid avoidable mistakes.

☐ Is the coordination completed?

☐ Have all key line and staff agencies had the opportunity to comment, criticize, or express their nonconcurrence on the options and recommendations?

☐ Do I have the authority to make this decision? If not, who does?

☐ Is this the right time to decide?

☐ Would postponing the decision help or hurt the mission of the organization?

☐ What will be the general reaction throughout my organization?
    —will it help or hurt morale?
    —will it undermine my legitimacy as the leader?
    —will it significantly enhance output or mission accomplishment?

☐ Has informal coordination with outside organizations taken place already? If not, should I telephone some key people to make sure that my decision doesn't receive too much negative reaction and criticism?

☐ How should this decision be announced?
    —at a press conference?
    —at a staff meeting?
    —by a decision letter?
    —by telephone calls to superiors and key subordinates?

☐ Does the statement announcing the decision include a complete rationale for the decision?

☐ Does this decision conform to my long-range plan?

☐ Is it faithful to my goals and priorities?

☐ Is it consistent with my previous decisions?

☐ If I am about ready to launch off in a new direction, do I need to change my long-range plan, my goals, or my priorities?

☐ Have I carefully weighed the five decision checks (pages 68–70)?
    —Sanity
    —Dignity
    —Systems
    —*Washington Post*
    —Integrity

12.   Executive Skills Checklist

Leaders and would-be leaders can improve their effectiveness, save a great deal of time, and improve their quality of life if they strive to enhance their leadership skills. This checklist can assist considerably in this regard. All leaders would do well to glance over this checklist at least once every six months.

☐ Are you skilled in giving dictation?
   —to your secretary?
   —to a dictaphone?

☐ Are you a speed reader? If not, do you plan to take a course in speed reading soon?

☐ Who arranges your schedule?
   —have you provided definitive guidelines on your schedule to your executive secretary or to your administrative assistant?
   —does your daily schedule have more than one event per hour? If so, are you over-scheduled?
   —do you have time to think, to write, to plan, to be introspective?

☐ In your yearly calendar, when do you plan to have your off-site seminar with key subordinates?
   —when do you plan to schedule your one-on-one session with key subordinates?
   —on what schedule do you plan to visit your geographically separated field organizations?
   —what is your vacation schedule?

☐ When was the last time you rewrote your philosophy letter?

☐ How current is your long-range plan?
   —how often are you meeting with the long-range planning division?
   —does your long-range planning division serve as a clearinghouse for new ideas and innovations?

☐ What is the quality, timing, and effectiveness of your organizational newspaper, magazine, or newsletter?
  —what kind of feedback mechanisms are available to measure its impact?
  —does it serve the mission directly, indirectly, or both?
  —what percentage of your subordinates read it?

☐ Who in your organization is totally frank with you?
  —what are the subordinates saying about you over a cup of coffee or at the bar?
  —which subordinates are sycophants?

☐ What are your major weaknesses as a leader? What are you doing to improve these weak areas?

☐ Are you perceived as:
  —out of touch?
  —past your prime?
  —authoritarian?
  —non-decisive?
  —a captive of your staff?
  —arrogant?
  —intense?
  —biased?
  —self-righteous?
  —lazy?
  —a micromanager?
  —an alcoholic?
  —lacking in style?
  —preoccupied?
  —aloof?
  —a philanderer or flirt?

☐ What are the means by which new ideas bubble up to the top in your organization?

☐ How many new ideas have been implemented in the past year?

☐ What legacy do you wish to leave behind you?

☐ Which subordinates are capable of replacing you?

13. Introspection Checklist

Introspection is an important part of leadership. Leaders who know who they are, who recognize their strengths and use them to advantage, and who understand and compensate for their weaknesses, have a tremendous advantage—they perform much better than leaders who do not or cannot understand themselves. This checklist provides a framework for objective introspection.

☐ Do you plan your weekly and monthly schedule carefully? Do you stick to it fairly closely?

☐ Does your executive secretary help you maintain your schedule?

☐ Have you established organizational priorities? Do you and your subordinates stick to these priorities consistently?

☐ How reliable are you? How many meetings, speeches, trips, social engagements, professional commitments, etc. have you cancelled during the past month?

☐ Who tells you all the news—good and bad?

☐ How long are your meetings?

☐ How well do you listen? Do you spend at least 75 percent of your time listening when you interact with others?

☐ Do people fear you, distrust you, like you, respect you, love you? How courteous are you?

☐ What is your body language like?

☐ Are you considered a communicator?

☐ Are you considered a disciplinarian?

☐ Do you enjoy your job?

☐ Are you flexible?

☐ Do you maintain physical and intellectual fitness?

- ☐ Are you a deflector of pressure from above or a magnifier of that pressure?
- ☐ Are you tuned in or out of touch?
- ☐ Are you a delegator?
- ☐ Are you a nondrinker, a drinker, an alcoholic?
- ☐ Are you an optimist or a pessimist?
- ☐ Are you religious? What are your ethics and values?
- ☐ Are you a writer?
- ☐ Are you ambitious?
- ☐ Are you secure or insecure?
- ☐ What is your integrity level?
- ☐ Are you an intense individual or are you relaxed?
- ☐ Are you decisive or are you a "decision ducker"?
- ☐ How "conceptual" are you?

---

14. Press Conference and Media Interview Checklist

With the explosive growth of the media in recent years, it is not just heads of state, foreign dignitaries, senators, governors, mayors, generals, and CEOs of major corporations that meet regularly with members of the media. Leaders at many levels must be prepared to interact, often on short notice, with reporters. This checklist can be a useful reminder as you prepare for your next press conference.

☐ Are you the correct person to face the press?
  —If not, can you pick someone else without being accused of ducking the press?

☐ Do you have a written statement to give or to read the media?
  —Have you studied it closely to be sure that it conforms to policy and that you are comfortable with it?

☐ Who will be there?
  —what are their backgrounds, biases, and reputations for fairness?

☐ Are any of the police-reporter type?

☐ Will the interview be on or off the record?

☐ If a press conference, how long will it last?
  —How will it be terminated?

☐ Will the TV cameras be there?
  —Will it be live or on tape?

☐ Will you get to see a copy of the manuscript or edited TV tape?

☐ What agenda do you wish to pursue?

☐ What have you or your organization done recently that is particularly noteworthy?

☐ What tough questions can you expect and on what issues?

　　—What are good answers to these questions?

☐ What issues are particularly sensitive ones for your boss?

☐ What mistakes have been made by spokespersons in your organization that you might wish to clarify or correct?

☐ What is your reputation with the press?

☐ What is your organization's reputation with the press?

☐ Are there any skeletons in your closet?

　　—If so, are you prepared if you are confronted with tough questions about your personal or professional conduct?

☐ If you expect a hostile session, what approach have you devised to reduce the hostility?

　　—Has your staff given you any suggestions?

　　—Have you considered the use of humor?

15. Planning Checklist

One major responsibility of the leader is to establish a strategic vision for the organization. A plans office and an institutionalized planning system can be helpful in this regard. Some useful questions about planning follow:

☐ What are your organization's plans?

☐ How large is the planning staff?

☐ Do they report directly to you? If not, why not?

☐ Is there a long-range plan?
—how is it used and by whom?
—if not, what is the strategic vision of your organization?

☐ Does your planning system include:
—personnel planning?
—resource planning?
—facility/construction planning?
—logistics planning?
—operational planning?
—contingency planning?
—opportunity planning?
—economic planning?
—investment planning?

☐ What is the staff relationship between the chief planner and
—the chief of personnel?
—the chief of logistics?
—the chief of finance?
—the chief of operations?
—the field organizations?

☐ What kind of divestiture and reevaluation of priorities is taking place?

☐ What major innovations are underway in your organization?

☐ How often is there a planning/innovation off-site seminar?

☐ Are there regular, scheduled meetings between you and your long-range planners? Do these meetings lead to any decisions?

☐ Who is responsible for carrying out any decisions that might impact on the long-range future of your organization?

☐ At what points in the future should I revisit each decision?

16. Divestiture Checklist

All large organizations will, over time, become obsolescent unless divestiture planning takes place on a regular basis. Opportunities should be actively sought to close down obsolete plants, to disestablish offices that no longer contribute significantly to the mission, to discontinue product lines that are losing market appeal, and to unload technologically obsolescent systems. The following questions can help leaders to highlight divestiture opportunities.

- ☐ What short-term and long-term impact will this divestiture opportunity have on the mission of the organization? Will the short-term disadvantages be outweighed by the long-term advantages?

- ☐ What are the principal advantages of this divestiture opportunity?

- ☐ What are the principal disadvantages of this divestiture opportunity?

- ☐ How much money, personnel, and other resources will be saved as a result of this divestiture? How easy will it be to transfer these resources into more productive areas?

- ☐ What impact will this divestiture have on the overall philosophy, priorities, and goals of this organization?

- ☐ Will the goals, priorities, and philosophy of the organization have to be changed as a result of this divestiture?

- ☐ Do I have the authority to make this decision myself?

- ☐ With whom should I consult before I make my decision?

- ☐ Should I call in an outside consultant to get a disinterested opinion on the wisdom of this divestiture proposal?

- ☐ What are the alternative means by which this divestiture can be implemented? Which is the best scheme?

☐ Which individuals will lose their jobs, and how involved should I be in counselling them and finding them attractive new job opportunities?

☐ Does this divestiture provide opportunities to do other important things, such as reorganization, removing incompetent employees, etc.?

☐ What are the various ways in which resources that are saved can be applied to other areas within the organization? Which is the best way?

☐ How will this divestiture be perceived by the employees throughout the organization? Will it be interpreted as being the first of a number of divestiture steps that may threaten many jobs throughout the organization?

☐ How should the decision be announced? Should I do it myself?

17. Meeting Checklist

This checklist should be helpful to executives, their immediate staffs, and to any corporate officer, factory manager, or division chief who is responsible for chairing meetings. The purpose of this checklist is to improve the effectiveness of the meeting environment while reducing the time and the frustrations of long, undisciplined meetings.

- ☐ What is the purpose of the meeting? What is the agenda?
- ☐ Who will be in attendance?
  - —have invitations been sent to all the corporate divisions, regional offices, international bureaus, factories, sales offices, etc.?
  - —is the chief lawyer in attendance or properly represented?
- ☐ How much time is allocated for the meeting?
  - —do any key players have to leave early? if so, who? should the agenda be adjusted accordingly?
  - —what plan do you have to keep the meeting on track?
- ☐ Who will be the recorder for the meeting?
  - —will there be minutes?
  - —will action items be committed to writing after the meeting?
- ☐ Are there presentations to be made?
  - —if so, by whom?
  - —are there time limits placed on each presentation?
  - —will there be enough time for adequate discussion?
- ☐ Will decisions be made during the meeting?
  - —if so, will you announce them at the end?
  - —if not, should you announce when and how decisions will be made?
- ☐ What is your meeting strategy?
  - —who are the main antagonists?

—is compromise possible? is compromise wise? will compromise lead to a watered-down solution?

☐ Who will be responsible for implementation of decisions?

☐ Will additional meetings be needed?
   —should these meetings be announced prior to the end of this meeting?
   —if not, will you announce that this is the final meeting on this subject?

☐ If key players cannot attend, can they be hooked up through a teleconference system or some other means?

☐ Do you have an overall policy on length of meetings, number of presentations, and length of presentations?
   —in this meeting, do you intend to hold to these constraints?
   —if not, do you intend to announce your position at the start of the meeting?

☐ Do you intend to run the meeting yourself or to allow someone else to chair the meeting?

18. Integrity Checklist

There are certain areas in organizations where integrity is tested often. It is important for the leader periodically to check these areas to ensure that high standards of integrity are being maintained.

- ☐ the inspection system.
- ☐ the training system.
- ☐ the management control system.
- ☐ the reporting system.
- ☐ the testing system.
- ☐ congressional testimony.
- ☐ submission of programs and budgets.
- ☐ training competitions.
- ☐ records within the personnel system.
- ☐ the bonus system.
- ☐ hiring practices.
- ☐ equal opportunity programs.
- ☐ expense accounts.
- ☐ perquisites.
- ☐ pressuring subordinates to join groups or make monetary contributions.
- ☐ inventory control and fund control in quasi-official clubs or organizations.
- ☐ covert operations, if any.

---

19. Promotion Board Checklist*

This checklist was created by Admiral J.S. Gracey when he was the Commandant of the Coast Guard.

To promotion board members: in selecting future leaders, ask yourselves the following questions about each person.

Is This Person:

- ☐ a self starter?

- ☐ willing to go out on a limb?

- ☐ willing to walk the extra mile?

- ☐ courteous and considerate, especially to/of juniors?

- ☐ a professional?

- ☐ biased in any way?

- ☐ afraid of making a mistake?

- ☐ socially active and adept? Is his or her spouse?

- ☐ strong only in his or her own "specialty," or can he or she contribute in the whole range of activities of the firm, service, or agency?

- ☐ willing to try new things, even at some risk?

- ☐ practical and realistic?

- ☐ warm and personable?

- ☐ capable of being a maverick? Does he or she always insist on being a maverick?

- ☐ perceptive?

- ☐ innovative?

Does This Person:

- ☐ tell me what he or she thinks, not tell me what he or she thinks I want to hear?

*Reprinted by permission of Admiral James S. Gracey, U.S. Coast Guard (Ret.).

- ☐ make service to his or her institution his or her number one priority despite personal sacrifice?
- ☐ have a love affair going with his or her organization?
- ☐ set a good example in all respects?
- ☐ think of the wants and needs of individuals and of their families?
- ☐ suffer from "Chicken Littleism"?
- ☐ meet the public well?
- ☐ get awed by "big wheels," or is he or she at ease with them?
- ☐ let concern for his or her "future" govern his or her actions?
- ☐ understand the government . . . how it works and how to work in it?
- ☐ understand Congress and how to work with congressmen and congresswomen?
- ☐ express himself or herself well, on paper and orally?
- ☐ understand the organization he or she serves?
- ☐ understand his or her institution's role in government and its relations with state and local governments?
- ☐ understand his or her institution's role in community and business affairs?
- ☐ make things happen?
- ☐ get things done?
- ☐ lead, not push?
- ☐ make a good team with his or her spouse in representing the institution he or she serves?
- ☐ have imagination?
- ☐ worry about who gets the credit?
- ☐ praise his or her people?

☐ go to bat for his or her people?

Will This Person:

☐ disagree with me when he or she thinks I am wrong?

☐ stand up and be counted?

Can This Person:

☐ "walk with kings, and not lose the common touch?"

☐ handle a huge workload and not lose the bubble?

☐ keep twelve oranges in the air at once and not drop any?

☐ accept the ideas of others?

☐ convey his or her ideas to others . . . and sell them?

☐ laugh at himself or herself?

☐ laugh at all . . . i.e., does he or she have a good sense of humor?

☐ deal with the press and other media?

☐ walk in another person's shoes, no matter how big or small?

☐ make a speech that people will listen to?

☐ sort out problems and keep his or her priorities straight?

☐ hit a golf ball in a shower stall and not get beaned?

☐ think on his or her feet?

☐ be tough when necessary?

☐ take an unpopular, but necessary, stand and stick to it?

☐ grasp new concepts quickly?

☐ identify problems (vs. symptoms) . . . and get them solved?

☐ find a new course if the one he or she has selected comes a cropper?

☐ get "lost" in the infamous, single-tree "impenetrable forest"?

☐ make decisions? *Does* he or she make them?

☐ handle pressure?

☐ inspire others?

Would I want to work with this person as a fellow leader?

Has this person got "class"?

20. Congressional Visit Checklist*

This checklist provides guidelines to be considered by the leader when a Member of Congress or a staff member from Congress is coming to visit his or her organization. The items here do not necessarily require action, but will remind the leader of those areas that he or she might wish to review or have his or her staff investigate prior to the congressional visit.

☐ Are you aware of the rights of congressional members; of the sense, the direction of the Congress in session?
—Congress is not the enemy.
—Members have a right to ask questions.
—Members and their questions deserve your timely response.
—it is important to know the current issues and emphases of Congress.

☐ Are you aware of the significance of the constituents and constituent interest?
—minimize briefings to Members.
—provide a list of people the Member met personally.
—emphasize the participation of women and minorities in your mission.

☐ Are you aware that it may be necessary to treat Members and staffers differently?
—personal staffers manage the Member's office.
—professional staffers work directly on legislation.
—staffers can be very influential with their Member.
—staffers are issue-oriented; they want detail.
—be truthful and objective.
—remember that briefings to staffers can be more lengthy than those to the Member of Congress.
—provide point papers and copies of charts.
—have experts at your briefings to brief and to answer questions.

*This checklist is a modification of one that was prepared by Wilson R. Rutherford, III, and Leslie F. Kenne.

—keep the number of your people at the briefings small.

—Members tend to be generalists, more interested in orientation than in details.

    —make briefings few and short.

    —provide overview of mission.

    —speak in layperson's terms; avoid acronyms.

    —give windshield and walking tours.

    —provide hands-on demonstrations.

—Members are usually interested in meeting constituents.

☐ Are you well aware of the issues to be discussed? Do you know what factors to consider in your discussion?

    —primary versus secondary issues.

    —your agenda versus that of your organization; the organization's agenda normally has higher priority.

    —the Washington agenda.

    —institutional priorities on issues.

    —the various sides of the issues.

    —the need to show things in a balanced way.

☐ Are you aware that your attitude is all-important to a successful visit?

    —be careful to avoid personality conflicts.

    —be responsive.

    —remain nonpartisan.

    —don't try to "snow" anybody.

    —be candid and honest.

    —caveat personal opinions.

    —don't shoot from the hip.

    —know the politics of the district/state.

    —put yourself in the Member's shoes.

    —be careful in advancing your own agenda.

    —be enthusiastic and positive.

☐ Have you coordinated the visit with appropriate agencies?

    —relied on the agency or corporate office for legislative affairs for guidance?

—obtained background information from corporate headquarters or legislative affairs in Washington?

—gotten local community leaders and government officials involved; cultivated their support?

—ensured functional area coordination between your office and corporate headquarters?

—let your boss know how the visit went; related any unplanned incident or major mistakes you have made?

21. Congressional Testimony Checklist

Because of the proliferation of Congressional committees and subcommittees, the tendency of Members of Congress to hold more and more hearings in Washington and around the country, and the proliferation of political issues (particularly in the financial, environmental, and social welfare areas), the chances of leaders being called upon to testify before Congress has increased dramatically. This checklist was developed after I had testified as a principal witness before many committees and subcommittees of both Houses of the United States Congress.

☐ Which committee or subcommittee?

☐ Which hearing room?

☐ Will the hearing be open or closed?
   —Will the hearing be televised?

☐ Which Members of Congress and key staffers are expected to attend?
   —What points of view, constituent interests and biases can I expect from each congressman or congresswoman, and from each key staffer?

☐ Which Members of Congress are likely to be hostile?
   —Why and on what issues?

☐ Are "prepared remarks" appropriate?
   —Have they been prepared?
   —Have they been submitted at least forty-eight hours ahead of time?
   —Are you ready to summarize the prepared remarks in a very few minutes?

☐ Are there any other principal witnesses?
   —Have you met with them ahead of time?
   —If not, can you arrange to meet them a few minutes ahead of time to coordinate on the testimony?

☐ Is there an opportunity to submit questions ahead of time that the chairperson or someone else might ask of you?

—If so, have the questions been submitted?
—Have you thought through the answers to these questions?

22. Rules of Thumb for Congressional Testimony

So many people who testify before the U.S. Congress fail to understand some basic factors. My rules of thumb may be helpful as you prepare for your first (or next) opportunity to testify on Capitol Hill.

☐ Never lie.
 —For two reasons: it is wrong and it is dumb. (You will surely get caught if you lie and once caught you will ruin your reputation with the Congress for the rest of your professional life.)

☐ Do not read your opening statement.
 —Submit it for the record and summarize it in three to five minutes.

☐ Be prepared.
 —Reading and skull sessions with your staff are very helpful.

☐ Give brief answers to the questions.

☐ Be respectful to Members of the Congress.
 —Although particular individuals may not be too sharp, the institution deserves your respect. An arrogant witness is seldom a successful witness.

☐ Be aware of specific constituency interests on the part of Members.

☐ Never arrive late to a hearing.
 —Better an hour early than five minutes late.

☐ As Members and staffers wander into the hearing room prior to the hearing, approach them, introduce yourself to them, and remind them where you have met before.

☐ Do not allow yourself to be intimidated.

—If a Member of Congress badgers you, listen quietly until the statement is over, and then, quietly but forcefully, state your position. Point out, in specific terms, where the Member may be in error.

☐ Do not interrupt a Member of Congress.

☐ If you don't know the answer to the question, tell the Member that you will submit the answer for the record.

☐ If you generally know the answer but you are not sure of all the details, do your best to answer it (If you say "I'll submit an answer for the record" too many times, you will not be a very credible or effective witness.)

☐ If you promise to do something while you are testifying (to conduct a study, to provide data, etc.), do it promptly.

☐ Be sensitive about time and schedule with the committee.

☐ Do not bring a large number of back-up witnesses.
—You will appear to be much more in charge if you testify alone.

23.   Some Short Phrases Useful for Leaders

Leaders can use short phrases to make a point, pay a compliment, ask for feedback, take the blame for failure, ease the level of tension, etc. The following is a list of phrases that executives may find helpful in dealing positively with subordinates, in making decisions, and in disciplining themselves.

- ☐ I don't know.
- ☐ How am I wasting your time?
- ☐ You are responsible for my success.
- ☐ I made a mistake.
- ☐ I was wrong.
- ☐ You're the best.
- ☐ Perhaps it is time to take another look at my position on that issue.
- ☐ It's six o'clock, let's all go home.
- ☐ Let's go on a jog together and we can discuss it—you can talk and I will breathe.
- ☐ Let's include the spouses in this.
- ☐ What good books have you read lately?
- ☐ I'll be gone a month, don't worry about giving me updates.
- ☐ Let's try it (let's go for it).
- ☐ Well it didn't work, but I'm sure glad to gave it a try!
- ☐ Give it to me straight, folks—what did I do wrong?
- ☐ Your wise counsel has been very useful. Please forgive me for not following it this time.
- ☐ Help me discipline my in-box; don't send me issues that you are competent to decide.

☐ Our great success was your success; please don't give me the credit.

☐ This setback was my fault. I just didn't give you the support you needed.

☐ I know some of you are uncomfortable with this decision. I will take full responsibility if we fail.

☐ I have become part of the problem, I am stepping down so someone less committed to the past can take over this dynamic organization.

☐ Let's get back to basics.

☐ First things first.

24. Useful Phrases for Confident Subordinates

Subordinates need to be frank and candid with their bosses or the organization will suffer. On the other hand, it is important at times to be quite diplomatic. Finding the right phrase and finding the right time to use it can be quite a challenge. Here are a few useful phrases for all seasons.

- ☐ Please tell me what to do, not how to do it.
- ☐ It just won't work.
- ☐ This initiative could be your legacy.
- ☐ The time to decide is now.
- ☐ History will judge us kindly [severely] if we do this.
- ☐ The Board of Directors will go bananas when they learn about this.
- ☐ The local [national] press sure will have fun with this one.
- ☐ I wonder which one of the departments will leak this story first?
- ☐ Let's go for it!
- ☐ Before we go with this I suggest we run it by our lawyer.
- ☐ Life's full of risks. So let's take one!
- ☐ If I do that for you, I won't be able to sleep at night.
- ☐ We can't afford *not* to do this.
- ☐ If we decide to do this, the folks on the floor will love [hate] you.
- ☐ If you decide to go this route you might just as well fire Sam [or Sue]; you will have destroyed his [or her] credibility with his [or her] employees.
- ☐ There ain't no way.
- ☐ It sure doesn't go along with our strategic plan.

☐ This will give us a big edge over our competition.

☐ It won't go down well on the production line.

☐ Of course, our competitors are doing it, but we have higher standards.

☐ If you want it bad you will get it bad; let's give the staff another week.

25. Thoughts For All Seasons

There are some truisms that can't be defined as rules of thumb but still are useful for leaders and subordinates to think about from time to time.

☐ *If you want it bad, you'll get it bad.*
A clever put-down for a subordinate who is trying to convince his or her boss that a short deadline will lead to poor results.

☐ *Perfect is the enemy of Good.*
When a leader seeks perfection, he or she often gets just the opposite. Very good solutions are often better than perfect solutions—particularly when the perfect solutions can't be found until three months too late. Very good solutions tend to be cheaper, faster, and easier to implement than perfect solutions.

☐ *"Sir, it's time to blow up the bridge."*
The Academy Award Winning movie of 1957, *Bridge on the River Kwai*, demonstrated with great clarity the dangers of rigid planning. It was correct for the British and American prisoners of war to build the bridge for their Japanese captors; it was also correct to blow it up when the Japanese train arrived. How often have we watched good policy evolve into bad policy—and yet find changing it awfully hard?

☐ *The paper is in the typewriter.*
A useful way to get a few more hours to polish up a staff paper. Only to be used when the paper has been written in draft form and is, in fact, being typed or put into the computer.

☐ *It won't go down on the production line.*
This idea, procedure, or approach may seem great in the corporate boardroom; but, if it won't work on the production line, in the field, or in the sales office, it's time to take another look at it.

APPENDIX B
case studies

Each of these case studies is true. Many happened to me and the rest occurred to friends or colleagues. They come from a number of sources: corporations, nonprofit organizations, the federal government, local government, and the military. Although the settings may be quite different, it is clear that leaders in one sector of a society can learn from the experiences of leaders in other sectors. The interactions of followers and leaders, the ethical dilemmas, the importance of mission, and the challenges facing the leader are often quite similar as one moves from one large organization to the next. I have purposely kept the cases and the analyses short to maximize their value for busy readers. The analyses appear in Appendix C (see page 233).

1. You are the head of an organization that is responsible for the maintenance of a large number of airplanes. There are 1,600 people working for you. One of your four subordinate leaders has shown indications of having considerable problems in working cooperatively with fellow leaders. In addition, you have observed that in the afternoons his speech is sometimes slurred. He seems to be using breath mints a great deal in the afternoons. You suspect that he may be drinking heavily at noontime and that he may have a drinking problem or be an alcoholic. You have no direct evidence or information and his people seem to be "protecting" him. As his immediate boss, what do you do?

2. You are the president of a large technical organization doing research for large corporations and for the government. You have been in business for four years and have grown dra-

matically each year. You have a line of credit with your bank for $16 million. It is the nature of your business that, largely because of time delays in getting paid by your clients, you are in the red until about the first of February and strongly in the black from then until the end of your fiscal year on 30 September. A few days before Christmas the president of your bank demands an urgent meeting.

You and your top corporate staff meet with him. He says that there are only $3 million left of your line of credit and that you must take draconian actions to ensure that you do not exceed the $16 million. You explain to him calmly that what is happening is normal for your kind of business and ask that an additional line of credit be established just in case you exceed the $16 million. The banker is adamant—he will not extend your line of credit and demands fast action. What do you do?

3. You are a fast-rising young executive in a very large corporation. The corporation's president has just called you in to tell you that he is going to send you out to a city on the Indian subcontinent as the president of a major subsidiary company. You will have over 600 people working for you, most of whom will be nationals of the host country. The president tells you in his normally indirect, nonspecific way that there are major problems "out there" and it is your job to fix them. Soon after you arrive you learn that a number of corporate officers there are involved in illegal activities (that are hugely profitable personally to these officials); you also find that the top foreign national in this subsidiary company is indirectly involved in these illegal activities. What do you do?

4. You are a president of a large industrial firm. You are having a counselling session with a senior vice president. After acknowledging all the fine contributions she has made to the company over the past year, you make a couple of modest criticisms of the way she has managed two small programs. She reacts very negatively and emotionally to your criticism and feels that you are wrong on both counts. What do you do?

5.   You are the president of a large overseas subsidiary of a multinational corporation and the local police have uncovered a marijuana ring that includes a number of high school students who are selling marijuana to their friends at the international high school where many of your employees send their children. One of the drug salesmen is a son of a plant manager who works directly for you. The other drug pushers are the sons and daughters of less senior officials in your company. What do you do?

6.   As a president of a major corporation that does a great deal of work for the Department of Defense, you are testifying on Capitol Hill. Just before you leave your Washington office, you learn of a major testing failure of the weapons system on which you are about to testify. You know the upcoming vote in the committee later that day will be very close. You are getting conflicting advice from your staff. You are quite sure that none of the committee members or the Congressional staff members are aware of the test failure. In your testimony, should you raise the issue of the test failure? If so, what do you say?

7.   You are the CEO of a major newspaper chain. The sports director of one of your papers has been arrested for child molestation. The judge has found the man guilty and has given him a heavy fine as well as a long jail sentence, both suspended. This man has been a brilliant reporter and sports director and has never been any kind of a problem. What do you do?

8.   You hired someone to start a new division in your company. He has the reputation of being the finest technical person in the country in a narrow but important new field. He asks before you hire him if he could do some teaching on the side. You agree, in an offhand manner, with his request. He brings on a team of five others and puts together a number of proposals for potential customers. Eighteen months later, you learn that this group has set up an independent company and is doing a great amount of teaching on the weekends and at night and is using company time to put the course materials together. The

team still seems to be working hard for you, but has yet to land a contract for your company. What do you do?

9. You have just arrived at an overseas location to take over a large subsidiary of your company. The parent company has just changed its management philosophy from hierarchical to matrix management and you will have to share power with a number of others. The culture of this overseas city is very much "old world," where the top boss is king. The people in this location have little experience in matrix management. What do you do?

10. You are the president of a medium-sized university that has an active and successful intercollegiate sports program. You go to almost all of the major sporting events held at your campus, including all the home football games, which usually draw a crowd of about 5,000 fans. In recent games you have noticed thirty or forty of your students dreaming up obscene cheers to taunt the opposition, as well as engaging in shoving matches with each other that once or twice have broken out into fist fights. What do you do?

11. You are the principal of a large suburban high school. The student president of the senior class, the most outstanding scholar in the entire school, has just committed suicide. What do you do?

12. You are the planning director of a large government agency in Washington. There are a large number of civil servants throughout the country who wish to serve in this department since promotion opportunities are very favorable there and the work is interesting. As a result, it is quite common for you to get a letter or phone call from a senior official recommending an individual. Over a period of about two months, you receive separate letters from seven senior officials recommending someone to come work for you. Do you hire this person?

13. You are an assistant secretary of a military department vis-

iting a major city in the Midwest. You have been asked by the Secretary to have a session with the editorial board of the major morning newspaper of this city. In the discussion one of the journalists presses you hard about why your service is not developing a weapons system to accomplish an important mission. You know of a program that, in fact, addresses that mission very well, but the technology is so sensitive that the whole program is highly classified and compartmentalized. How would you handle this line of questioning?

14. You are the mayor of a medium-sized city (about 200,000 people). A member of your fire department has accused another member of cheating on the examination that would, if passed, take him to the next rank. An investigation takes place and the result is a recommendation that the accused individual, whom the investigation team felt had cheated, be suspended for a year. The fire commission, which you appointed, has two basic options: to suspend the individual immediately or wait sixty days for a court to review the case. You, as mayor, have no direct jurisdiction over the commission, but you can give it advice. Early one morning the head of the fireman's union charges into your office and demands that the suspension be withheld until the court makes its judgment. He also threatens to take all the fire equipment in the entire city and park it in front of City Hall if he does not get his way. As mayor, what do you do?

15. You are an Air Force commander in Europe and you have five Tactical Fighter, Tactical Reconnaissance, and Tactical Control Wings under your command. The wings have from 4,000 to 7,000 people and each wing is commanded by a colonel. One of the wing commanders has recently been promoted to general officer and will be leaving shortly. The vice wing commander of this wing is very well qualified, has been in the wing for two years, and is the logical choice to move up to become the commander. You have heard informally that the vice wing commander's wife has psychiatric problems that are causing morale problems among the wives of the officers in the wing.

(For instance, she has been heard to say to wives of young officers, "I'll have your husband fired.") However, the vice commander refuses to acknowledge that his wife needs psychiatric care. What do you do?

16.   You are a wing commander of an overseas fighter wing and in the last few months you have lost three F–15 aircraft to accidents and one pilot has been killed. Morale in the wing is low as a result and the wing has lost some confidence in itself. The chief of maintenance comes forward to you with a proposal that the wing attempt to establish a new all-time record for sortie production in a 24-hour period by flying 450 individual aircraft flights in a single day. The record for a fighter wing in Europe is 296 sorties. Available to fly are sixty aircraft and seventy pilots. What do you do?

17.   You are commander of a large ship in the United States Navy. You receive a call from the wife of one of the officers on your ship. She tells you that a "contract" has been arranged and a certain officer on the ship will soon be murdered. The telephone caller had overheard a telephone conversation between her next-door neighbor and someone else. It was clear that the next-door neighbor was setting up an arrangement to have her husband killed in order to collect his insurance money; she has already given the two "hit" men a down payment by check. The wife who was calling you seems to have rather detailed information on where and when the murder will take place. What do you do?

18.   You are the deputy wing commander for maintenance in a fighter wing in Europe. After you have been in your position for a few weeks you uncover the fact that your midnight shift has been submitting a daily report at 3:00 a.m. to higher headquarters showing more aircraft in operationally ready status than are in that status at that hour. When you question this practice you are told that this has been going on for some time. It helps the wing and the wing commander look good to higher headquarters. Normally, by 7:00 a.m. that number of airplanes

is, in fact, available at a fully operational ready status for training (or combat) missions. What do you do?

19. You are a commander of a large military unit in the Philippines. One morning on the police blotter you notice that a technical sergeant has been picked up for drunken driving at the main gate (driving erratically and having the odor of alcohol on his breath). A week later the police blotter reports the blood test "positive" for amphetamines, but reports no trace of alcohol. What do you do?

APPENDIX C
analysis of case studies

The following paragraphs outline the action that was taken for each of the case studies highlighted in Appendix B. A brief discussion covers the actions taken by the leader. In some cases, the discussion is followed by a brief analysis of the strengths and weaknesses of the solution picked by the leader to handle this problem, as well as lessons learned from this experience. (All of these events occurred; in some cases, the circumstances have been modified slightly to avoid embarrassing anyone.)

1.   The individual clearly had a problem, but for some months he was so careful and so secretive about his drinking problem that it was hard to pinpoint specific incidents where he was drinking or drunk on the job. The subordinate leader's administrative assistant was called in by the leader. She was told that her boss might be an alcoholic; yet, the leader couldn't put his finger on it and needed her to track his behavior and his whereabouts. She agreed to do this. For the next month or two she was able to keep a record, just for the use of the leader, showing where her boss was and when and whether he showed signs of drinking during the day. She brought the report back to the leader; it showed clearly that the boss was drinking heavily at noontime. Sometimes he would not return to work. If he did return, he would close his door; he would not conduct business in the afternoon, but would instead sit quietly in his office. After receiving this report, the leader called in the subordinate leader at mid-afternoon.

   The leader told him that he thought he had a drinking problem, and asked him to go immediately to the hospital to take a blood test to see what his blood alcohol level was and to get advice and counsel from the medical specialists in the hospital. The blood tests showed that although he had a very low level of alcohol in his blood, he did have liver damage and was clearly a man suffering from alcohol abuse. He was sent to an alcohol rehabilitation program at a hospital 100 miles away. After four weeks he returned to his position.

The involvement of the administrative assistant who worked directly for the subordinate leader was probably inappropriate; the leader himself should have tracked the activities of his subordinate. Sending him to alcohol rehabilitation and leaving him in his position after rehabilitation was an appropriate action. Alcoholism is a disease and it was important for the man's self-esteem and for the self-esteem of other people who might be suffering from drinking problems to realize that there is no punishment involved in the treatment of people with alcohol problems. A second mistake the leader made, however, was taking many months to figure out that there was a problem.

2.   The leader took the steps required to avoid exceeding the line of credit. By late February, the company was in great shape, and by April it had paid back the entire $16 million. Later that summer, the leader fired the banker. He picked a bank that understands his business and keeps him informed well in advance about any concerns the bank may have. The lesson here is that a company must have a close relationship with its bank or banks, and that understanding, good communication, mutual respect, and trust should be the ground rules on all sides.

3.   The leader, by working closely with his top lawyer and the senior American in the headquarters and by coordinating with the local police, was able to indict a number of the company officials. They later received jail terms. He also called in the top foreign national and told him that it was time for him to accept early retirement and the man accepted this. The major mistake that the leader made was not developing a coherent public relations approach. As a result, the leader and the company suffered from an extensive period of bad press that might have

been avoided, at least in part. The lesson here may be that when a leader has to take very strong action, including sending his or her own employees to jail, a team of trusted associates needs to be assembled to ensure that the operational, legal, equal opportunity, public affairs, and integrity issues are addressed in a coordinated fashion.

4. This experience was very difficult because, despite all the soothing language of the leader, the vice president blew up. The leader was never able to convince her that he had raised a legitimate point or two in their discussions. It turned out that the vice president was extremely sensitive to criticism and was not able to weigh objectively constructive criticism. Further checking on the part of the leader revealed that this person had problems in productively relating to others. The counselling session had uncovered a part of her personality of which the leader had not been aware. The lesson here is that a leader should not be afraid to criticize; criticism may uncover more than you might expect.

5. In this case, the plant manager was confronted directly in order to find out the background of the situation and what he would be willing to do about it. He was quite cavalier about it and felt that it was not that big a problem—that lots of kids were "doing drugs." The leader asked the son and the father to attend a drug rehabilitation program in order to ensure that they fully understood the consequences of drug involvement. If the plant manager had not been willing to attend drug rehabilitation with his son, he would have been sent home. The lesson here is that it doesn't matter what position you hold; there will be opportunities for the children and spouses of senior people to get in trouble with drugs, theft, vandalism, and so forth. It is important for a leader to make it clear that major subordinate leaders have an even greater responsibility than others to set and maintain high standards for themselves and for members of their families. This is particularly true in overseas areas.

6.   The leader should and did raise this issue and gave as much
information to the committee as he had available on the test
failure. He did this for a number of reasons. First, it would be
wrong to withhold important information from a duly consti-
tuted congressional committee. Second, by withholding information, the leader would take the considerable risk of losing
credibility and trust. At a later point, committee members and
staffers might learn that there had been a failure and that the
president had had some information about it prior to his testimony that day. It is important to realize that the movement of a
program through the Congress is a long and complex process
that continues over a number of years. There are lots of opportunities for the Congress to withhold funds or cancel the program. A short-term victory often leads to a long-term defeat if
the victory is gained through manipulation of the facts or withholding of information. Members of Congress and congressional staffers have long memories, and individuals who testify on
Capitol Hill should realize that their most important assets are
credibility and truth.

7.   The CEO fired the individual for publicly embarrassing the
newspaper and the publishing company. Many months later the
fired reporter approached the CEO and told him that he had
spent all his severance pay, that he could not find a job, and that
he was destitute and desperate for work. After thoughtful consideration, the CEO called the editor of one of his periodicals in
a distant location and asked that the editor to give the man
another chance. He explained the entire situation to the editor
and asked that he not tell the other employees so that the man
could get a fresh start. The man settled down in his new job and
got married. He and his wife later had a baby. There was never
again a problem of sexual deviation. The lesson here is that in a
very high visibility industry like public service or the media,
very strong action is called for. On the other hand, the CEO felt
compassion for a talented man who under the influence of alcohol had made a terrible mistake. The period where the reporter was completely out of work was a very sobering one and
he has now found a new and happy life thanks to the actions of

a mature CEO who was willing to give someone a second chance.

8.   The CEO called in the division chief and explained to him that there seemed to be a clear conflict of interest here and that he must ask him to give up this independent business and spend his full time on company business. The employee said that he couldn't do that but that he was willing to discuss the options available. After some discussion where the employee stuck with his position of keeping his independent company going, the CEO said, "I think you have just resigned and I think I have just accepted your resignation." The lesson here is clear. When hiring new employees and especially ones who will be in leadership positions, it is important to make very specific what the work rules will be. It is best to put these rules in writing so there can be no misunderstanding on either side. The CEO, by agreeing to "some teaching on the side," made a mistake. Since this was a brand new enterprise it would have been better to ask the division chief to put all his efforts into his work and only do outside things after he had won some contracts. The employee, by using so much of the company's time and resources to support his independent business, also made a mistake. The whole enterprise cost the company about a million dollars with no positive results. The CEO said it was his worst mistake in ten years of running the company.

9.   This leader found he had a major task. He had to explain the new approach to all his employees through the process of meetings, written memos, training sessions, etc. He had to explain the system to all his major customers (many of whom not only didn't understand it but were also uncomfortable with this approach). This education process went on for years and only over an extended time did understanding and support evolve. The lesson here is that the cultural environment of an overseas subsidiary does not change easily and top executives must be careful not to design a management model that may work well in Chicago or Los Angeles but may not function as well in New Delhi or Rio.

10. The university president approached these individuals, sat down among them and began to talk to them in a friendly way. He let them know that he was interested in their having a good time but that he would be with them for the rest of the game. It soon became clear that they were willing to be more careful about what they said and what they did. The fact that some of them knew what the president had written in the university newspaper about decorum and conduct at football games helped. The president later wrote additional articles in the newspaper on this subject. Although the problem did not completely go away, it did diminish during the rest of the season. The lesson learned here is that whenever you have a large number of people congregating at a sporting event, there is always the possibility of drinking before the game, violation of the no-alcohol rule in the stadium, and harassment of the other team, its cheerleaders, or its fans. The president, or a senior university official who is well known in the university community, should attend major sporting events and intervene diplomatically but firmly in any situation that looks like it is beginning to get out of hand. This technique is also useful in identifying certain troublemakers so they can be subsequently disciplined.

11. The principal immediately activated the crisis response team of the school district and his own crisis response team. She got on the public address system and explained what she knew about the situation and gave the students some free time to get together to discuss the situation. She worked very closely with the parents on the funeral and memorial events. She volunteered to participate in the funeral and to give the eulogy. She suggested that a memorial and a scholarship be set up in the student's honor and helped with the fund drive. The lessons here are that at the time of a totally unexpected tragedy, as was the case here, the followers expect a great deal of the leader. The leader must drop all his or her daily activities and act quickly, decisively, and compassionately.

12. Clearly, this individual was spending a great deal of his

time working on his own future assignment in a very ambitious and "careerist" way by asking all those officials to go to bat for him at the same time. As a result, it was evident that he was not spending a great deal of his time concentrating on his present job. All the officials were sent letters by the planning director thanking them for their interest, but all were informed that the individual had not been selected to work in the department. The lesson learned from this case is that those individuals in government who are so interested in getting just the right assignment sometimes "shoot themselves in the foot" by coming across as being hyperambitious and unwilling to allow the personnel system to weigh the needs and desires of both the organization and the individual in finding appropriate assignments. Hyperambition hurts many very talented people; leaders should occasionally caution their subordinates, collectively and, when appropriate, individually, about not getting caught in the trap of careerism.

13. You are in a very delicate area here. It is important to be forthright with the media while, at the same time, guarding very sensitive and highly classified information. The assistant secretary answered it in the following way: "This is an area that we have great concern about and we are pursuing a number of technological solutions in hopes of developing a weapons system that will fill this gap." If the reporter continues to press for information, the best approach is probably to follow up by saying that "These technologies are of such a sensitive nature that it would be inappropriate for me to comment further on the specifics."

14. The mayor picked up the phone in his office and handed it to the head of the fireman's union. He told him to go ahead and call the fire stations as he had threatened to do but to be sure to tell everyone that those who participated in this illegal action would be fired *permanently.* He gave the union boss another choice—to sit down and discuss this issue calmly and rationally. The union boss, after expressing his views in rather colorful language, sat down with the mayor. The mayor in turn

talked to the commission; the suspension was withheld and the crisis was averted. A new and more professional examination was designed and a more foolproof examination system was created. The professionalism of the entire fire department was enhanced. The lesson here is: as a leader, don't allow yourself to be intimidated. When someone tries to bully you, be ready with a strong countervailing approach.

15.   Here is a case in which an Air Force two-star general received many indications that a vice commander's wife, because of psychiatric illness, was creating morale problems among the junior officers and their wives in the wing. The vice wing commander was not selected to become a wing commander. He returned to the United States and retired shortly thereafter. The mistake made in this case was that the numbered Air Force commander did not talk to the wing commander on the scene; he could have received some good advice from that individual. Rather than rejecting a well qualified man, the Air Force commander might have given the vice wing commander an opportunity to command the wing on a probationary basis, if he agreed to have his wife seek psychiatric care, or perhaps return to the States. This was a judgment call; since there were so many people who were well qualified to be wing commanders, the problem with the spouse was apparently enough to cause the general to choose someone else.

16.   In this case it was clear that a morale boosting exercise would be very helpful to both the maintenance people and the pilots. The commander set some general guidelines: meaningful training must take place on every sortie; safety had to be a primary concern, and the whole exercise had to be carefully planned and executed. The chief of maintenance and the director of operations sat down and came up with a reasonable number of sorties for a 24-hour day. After some coordination and debate, it was agreed that 325 sorties would be the goal. Each of the pilots who were scheduled for daytime flights were limited to a maximum for six sorties; the night pilots were limited to a maximum of four sorties. It turned out to be an ex-

traordinary day that boosted morale, particularly on the part of the maintenance people, who were very motivated by the fact that the airplanes were flying a lot and doing well. The maintenance people were absolutely delighted when, at the end of the day, the wing ran out of pilots in the twenty-second hour, had flown 322 sorties, and yet had forty-nine aircraft still "mission capable" and ready to fly. There were no accidents or incidents during the entire day and very few mistakes were made. If there is a lesson to be learned from this it is that setting meaningful records is a very useful motivational tool. It also proves to people that they can do more than they thought they could—a valuable lesson for a combat unit.

17. The commander called in a small group of his staff, as well as the FBI, to do some preliminary investigation of this situation and to give the commander advice. When it became clear that the facts substantiated the information of the telephone caller, the commander called in the officer and quietly laid out the situation to him. Although the officer initially did not believe the commander, when all the facts were known he changed his mind. The FBI set a trap and the officer went to the spot where the murder was to take place. The two men were apprehended and three individuals, including the officer's wife, were indicted for, and convicted of, attempted murder and sent to jail.

18. The deputy wing commander for maintenance approached the wing commander the next day and explained quite bluntly that the wing was sending a false and misleading official report to higher headquarters and to the Joint Chiefs of Staff. He explained to the wing commander that he thought this was wrong, and, in addition, that it was not in the interest of the wing. By reporting accurately, there was a better chance of getting supply and manpower support to solve the underlying problem of low readiness. He suggested to the wing commander that, starting the next morning, the report be made honestly and that the wing commander call the higher headquarters to let them know why the readiness status would be

dropping so dramatically. The wing commander readily agreed. The deputy wing commander for maintenance then called a meeting of his senior maintenance team (both officers and noncommissioned officers). He explained to them that it was wrong, and was not in the interest of the maintenance organization of the wing or the wing commander, to overstate combat capability. The nice thing about this story was there was no objection on the part of either the wing commander or the maintenance leaders to returning to a system of honest reporting.

19.   The commander called in his chief of security police and his hospital commander and told them that he thought something was strange. He asked them to investigate the situation to try to determine why someone with alcohol on his breath showed no alcohol in his blood. A few days later the hospital commander and security chief returned to outline the results of their investigation. The technical sergeant, having been driven home by the security police after the blood alcohol test, approached his next-door neighbor, who was also a sergeant. He told his neighbor that he was very concerned about losing his license for a year as a result of driving while intoxicated. He was also concerned that his wife, who did not drive, would have no way to get to work. The next-door neighbor suggested that both individuals go to the hospital that night and see if they could negotiate a blood swapping deal with the medical corpsman at the hospital. They were able to do that, but the next-door neighbor failed to mention that he had been using amphetamines. In this case, disciplinary action was taken against all three individuals involved in this scam. Mistakes that were made, however, were the following: the wing commander failed to call in the technical sergeant's squadron commander; in addition, the squadron commander, the hospital commander, and the chief of security police all failed to note the discrepancy, on the police blotter, in the blood alcohol test when the results became known. The major lesson here is that the police blotter will tell you a lot if it is read carefully by the commander and the subordinate commanders.

APPENDIX D
leadership education programs

I am a great believer in formal education for leaders and future leaders. I am particularly taken by programs that accomplish a great deal in a fairly short time. I would like to recommend a few of the very best programs that are available in the United States. All of these I am quite familiar with and recommend without qualification. Each of these programs provides opportunities for growth, introspection, and insight. They also provide fine opportunities for attendees to get to know one another. The learning among the students is one of the major advantages of each. Anyone in a leadership position, or anyone expecting to move into a leadership post in the next few years who has not already attended one of these programs should try hard to do so. It will be an invaluable experience.

The Kellogg National Fellowship Program was established in the late 1970s and provides a three-year, part-time scholarship program to people in this country who have a high potential for top leadership. Between forty and fifty men and women are selected each year out of about 1,000 applicants. Varying in age from the early thirties to the mid forties, these mature people have already demonstrated a desire to lead people. They are selected by a team of distinguished individuals who not only screen each application carefully but also interview the most qualified 100 or so candidates. Each new group assembles for the first time each June at the Spring Hill convention center west of Minneapolis for a week of orientation and education on leadership. It has been my pleasure in recent years to be one of the kickoff speakers at Spring Hill. Each fellow must choose a learning plan and study a leadership issue in an area completely outside his or her chosen profession. Over the course of the next three years, the group gets together about every six months for a one- or two-week session (including a two-week session in an overseas nation). Each fellow is given sufficient funds to buy a personal computer and to do research on the learning plan. In addition, the fellow's employer is reimbursed, in part, by the Foundation for some of the costs of the time lost from the job by each fellow. The Foundation also pays for the modem and the telephone costs that allow all the fellows to internet through their personal computers.

The American Leadership Forum, based in Houston, Texas, got its start in the early 1980s because of the pioneering spirit of Joe Jaworski. Jaworski, a successful lawyer in Houston, was profoundly saddened by the events surrounding Watergate, many of which he agonized over with his father, who was the Special Prosecutor. Joe Jaworski felt something needed to be done in this country to increase the commitment of citizens of high talent and high standards to leadership in the public sector.

He has a program in three cities, with plans to expand by the early 1990s to ten or more cities. Each city's annual program picks twenty outstanding community leaders and gives them a one-year experience consisting of twenty-five days of scheduled activity. The program starts out in the mountains of Colorado with a six-day outdoor experience that stresses not personal goals but group achievement. This week in the mountains breaks down many of the barriers that may have previously existed within the community (many of the fellows know each other before the program starts because of the fact that they hold leadership positions in the same community). After the week in the mountains, once or twice a month the group gets together to address a specific aspect of leadership or to work on a group project that the team itself has picked. The program ends up with a few days in Washington, DC, including a graduation ceremony. Usually the group project carries on beyond the end of the one-year program. There is a fee for this program, but it is waived in many cases. Joe Synan, the President of the ALF, explains that each community program must be self-sustaining and must be supported by the city leaders.

The Center for Creative Leadership at Greensboro, North Carolina, has a well deserved reputation for excellence. Started in the early 1970s with a generous long-term commitment from the Smith Richardson Foundation, the CCL has grown to a staff of about 150, about one-fourth of whom are involved in research. The Center is particularly strong in the behavioral sciences; the psychological testing and evaluation program is one of the very best in the world. The Center has a variety of programs that last from four to six days, several of which focus on creativity and innovation in organizations. Many are held at the modern and marvelously equipped facility at Greensboro, while others are held at various locations throughout the country and overseas. Under Walt Ulmer's enlightened leadership and with such superb staff members such as David Campbell, the future of CCL is extremely bright.

The Center for Reflective Leadership at the Hubert Humphrey Institute at the University of Minnesota has done some excellent work in three areas: First, in trying to create a general field theory about leadership, the Center has conceptualized quite well about the various subcategories of leadership. Second, the Center has also done a great deal with communities to try to enhance the quality and cooperation of leaders and leadership groups. This work has been largely in the state of Minnesota, but the Center has also reached out to communities in other states. Third, the Center has an excellent program for leaders from other nations; these leaders come to Minneapolis for a year of study and research. Although this center is quite small, it has accomplished a great deal during its short history.

The Military has some excellent programs at the various service academies and war colleges as well as at the command and staff colleges. In addition, each of the services has a leadership center: the Navy at Norfolk, Virginia; the Army at Fort Leavenworth, Kansas; the Air Force at Montgomery, Alabama; and the Marine Corps at Quantico, Virginia. In addition, the services do research on leadership; for instance, the Army Research Institute in Alexandria, Virginia has an active program of research on leadership both at the small unit level and at the executive level. Although the military programs are generally closed to people outside the federal government, many civilian employees of the federal government have opportunities to attend the war colleges. In addition, the military sponsors research on leadership with many universities and research centers.

The *Federal Executive Institute* at Charlottesville, Virginia has a strong four-week program on executive leadership and 600 of the best of the middle-level civilians in the government graduate from the Institute each year. The Director, Dr. Mike Hansen, as a strong background in executive development and has implemented some new programs since he took over in 1987.

The Center for Excellence in Government in Washington, DC has a small but very high-quality program called Business and Government Dialogues. Outstanding senior executive service (SES) professionals from the federal government are invited to participate in a dialogue with someone who has served at a high position in government and is now in a very senior position in the business world. The seminars are kept quite small— about 15—and last half a day. The businessman or woman will make an informal opening statement and, for the rest of the session, the participants share problems, solutions, and insights. The SES professionals from across government get a chance to know and learn from each other.

These programs are but a few of the many leadership education and executive development programs that are available to leaders and would-be leaders. Most colleges and universities, many management consultant firms, a number of chambers of commerce, and numerous community groups conduct executive development programs for leaders from many areas of American society. Many of these programs are specifically designed to attract leaders from diverse backgrounds. The purpose is not only to allow much of the learning to take place among the students but also to help leaders within a city, a region, or a community to know and understand one another better. Even those leaders who feel they do not need these programs should participate in them upon occasion—as much for the contacts they make and the contributions they can provide to others—as for what they can learn themselves. If successful leaders are willing to help other leaders and would-be leaders who do not have the same skills, experience, and wisdom, the nation will be well served.

APPENDIX E
Selected Bibliography

All the known world, excepting only savage nations, is governed by books.

—Voltaire

How many a man has dated a new era in his life from the reading of a book.

—Henry David Thoreau

The literature on leadership is rich and diverse. Those individuals interested in reading in the area of leadership are often at a loss finding the books that are the most relevant to the leadership challenges and opportunities facing them. This bibliography highlights those books that should be particularly helpful to leaders of large organizations.

Bennis, Warren, and Nanus, Burt. *Leaders: The Strategy of Taking Charge.* (New York: Harper and Row, 1985).

Bennis' insights on the role of the leader in infusing organizations with energy, in creating a culture of pride, in teachership, in the empowerment of subordinate leaders, and in avoiding activities that waste people's time are all quite persuasive. His careful research of many successful businessmen has uncovered an interesting statistic: almost all are happily married to their first wives.

Blanchard, Kenneth, and Johnson, Spencer. *The One-Minute Manager.* (New York: William Morrow and Company; 1982).

This short book is a quick read that has some useful insights into the value of delegating.

Burns, James McGregor. *Leadership*. (New York: Harper and Row, 1978).

This Pulitzer Prize and National Book Award winning book concentrates on political leadership. Burns' discussion of transactional and transforming leadership is tremendously insightful. For those readers who don't have time to read the entire work, I recommend those portions that focus on transforming leadership.

Campbell, David P. *If I Am in Charge Here, Why Is Everybody Laughing?* (Greensboro, NC: Center for Creative Leadership, 1984).

This book offers a delightful quick read with lots of useful insights.

Clausewitz, Karl von. *On War,* translated by Michael Howard and Peter Paret. (Princeton, NJ: Princeton University Press, 1976).

This classic on strategy has a particularly insightful chapter on military genius (pages 100—112) which should be mandatory reading for all students of leadership.

Grothe, Mardy, and Wylie, Peter. *Problem Bosses: Who They Are and How to Deal With Them.* (New York: Fawcett Crest Press, 1987).

This short and very readable book provides helpful hints about how to deal with a weak boss, including taking a stand, going over the boss's head, and "firing the boss."

Morris, Edmond. *The Rise of Theodore Roosevelt.* (New York: Coward, McCann, and Geoghegan, 1979).

This elegant and insightful political biography gives insights into the maturation and intellectual development of one of America's greatest leaders. Readers who dive into this book will quickly understand why President Ronald Reagan chose Morris to be his biographer and gave him personal access to the White House during the last three years of his administration.

Nye, Roger H. *The Challenge of Command: Readings for Military Excellence.* (Wayne, NJ: Avery Publishing Group, 1986).

A marvelous guide to the best books in the field of military leadership; must reading for all military professionals.

Peters, Tom, and Austin, Nancy. *A Passion for Excellence: The Leadership Difference.* (New York: Random House, 1985).

I particularly recommend the first and last parts of this study of leadership in the business world.

Pogue, Forrest. *George C. Marshall,* 4 vols. (New York: Viking Press, 1963, 1966, 1973, 1987).

This four-volume series is the finest biography of an American military leader available. The best volume is the second one. George Marshall, a man of towering moral authority, is someone well worth emulating.

Rosenbach, William E., and Taylor, Robert L. *Contemporary Issues in Leadership.* (Boulder, CO: Westview Press, 1984).

This is a carefully selected group of the finest articles written on leadership.

Shaara, Michael. *The Killer Angels.* (New York: David McKay Co., 1974).

This is probably the best historical novel on leadership available in print today. Happily, the novel is about 98 percent accurate. Only the specific words uttered by Lee, Longstreet, and others are not and cannot be historically precise.

Wareham, John. *Secrets of a Corporate Headhunter.* (New York: Atheneum Press, 1980).

This analysis of leadership from the unique perspective of a headhunter provides a kind of "street-smart," "gloves off" perspective. Particularly insightful is Chapter Eight, "How to Fire and Still Be Friends."

ABOUT THE AUTHOR

Perry Smith has led a number of large organizations, both in the United States and in Europe. He developed a course on leadership when he was the Commandant of the senior professional school for civilians and military leaders in the government of the United States, the National War College in Washington, DC. After the first version of this book became such a great success in the war colleges, command and staff colleges, and military academies, he decided to revise it for a larger audience. He has interviewed many top leaders in the business, nonprofit, government, and university worlds. Each of these executives had read the earlier version and was able to help with very specific suggestions for expansion and improvement. The result is a book for many audiences.

Perry Smith has flown 180 combat missions over North Vietnam and Laos; has commanded the F–15 equipped fighter wing at Bitburg, Germany; has been the Director of Plans for the United States Air Force; has led a large staff of officers and noncommissioned officers from five nations in Northern Germany; and has run a prestigious academic institution. His doctoral dissertation for Columbia University won the American Political Science Association Helen Dwight Reid award for the best dissertation in the fields of international relations, international organization, and international law.

He watched the Japanese drop bombs on Pearl Harbor as a six-year-old boy on his way to Sunday school and began lecturing at age seven when he returned to the United States and was the only one in his school who had seen war at first hand. He spends a lot of time on the lecture circuit today, speaking on such subjects as leadership, planning, strategy, ethics, and NATO. In recent years he has lectured in London, Rio de Janeiro, Tokyo, and Beijing, as well as in many locations in the

253

United States. He is on the advisory group for the Kellogg National Fellowship Program.

Perry Smith has written three books, including *Creating Strategic Vision,* a recently published book on long-range planing. *The Puzzle Palace: A Guide to the Pentagon* will be published in 1989. He and his wife live in the McLean, Virginia area. He is a member of the Order of Daedalians and the Council on Foreign Relations.

INDEX

ORDER FORM

Avery Publishing Group
• 350 Thorens Ave. •
Garden City Park, NY 11040

TAKING CHARGE
making the right choices

Please send me _____ copy(ies) of **Taking Charge: Making the Right Choices** at $10.95 per copy. Add $2.00 for shipping and handling. Make check or money order payable to Avery Publishing Group, Inc.

☐ Check Enclosed   ☐ P.O. attached
Charge my   ☐ Visa   ☐ MasterCard

VISA   **MasterCard**

_____   _____
Account Number (include all digits)   Card Expires (Mo./Yr.)

_____
Signature

Please send the book(s) I have requested to:

_____
Name (please print)

_____
Organization (if appropriate)

_____
Address

_____
City   State   Zip

Bulk purchase discounts are available.
For more information, call 1–800–548–5757. Allow two to three weeks for your book shipment to arrive.